THE NATIONAL GUARD IN POLITICS

✦   ✦   ✦   ✦   ✦   ✦   ✦   ✦

HARVARD POLITICAL STUDIES · PUBLISHED UNDER
THE DIRECTION OF THE DEPARTMENT OF GOVERNMENT
IN HARVARD UNIVERSITY

THE

NATIONAL GUARD

IN POLITICS

MARTHA DERTHICK

✦ ✦ ✦ ✦ ✦ ✦ ✦ ✦ ✦

HARVARD UNIVERSITY PRESS

CAMBRIDGE, MASSACHUSETTS · 1965

ACKNOWLEDGMENTS

My heaviest debt is to Samuel P. Huntington. He interested me in military politics in the first place, suggested a study of the Guard, and gave advice and support generously from start to finish.

The American Association of University Women supported research with a Mary E. Voigt Fellowship in 1959–60.

Officers and employees of the National Guard Association were extremely kind as hosts and helpful as sources of information. I am particularly grateful to Major General Ellard A. Walsh (Retired) for use of the diaries he kept as president of the Association and to Brigadier General Mark H. Galusha, director of the Association's staff, who let me make its headquarters mine.

The late V. O. Key, Jr., was my advisor during preparation of the manuscript as a doctoral dissertation at Radcliffe College, and, until illness prevented, he continued to offer advice as it was rewritten for publication. He always did so with patience, care, compassion, and wisdom.

I received help of many kinds from many others, including help with typing from Dartmouth College and the Department of Political Science at Stanford University. I have singled out those whose assistance was crucial to completion of the manuscript in its present (or any) form.

I would like to thank two others to whom my debt is more general but likewise heavy. My father, Everest P. Derthick, began years ago to teach me, as much by example as exhortation, that words in sequence ought to make sense, and if those that follow do, much of the credit belongs to him. Edward C. Banfield had no connection with this book, but I was associated with him during much of the time the manuscript was in preparation, and its shortcomings are much fewer on that account. What is more important, my enjoyment and understanding of political science are very much greater.

The Free Press of Glencoe, Illinois, which published some of my material on the Guard in Samuel P. Huntington, ed., *Changing Patterns of Military Politics* (1962), consented to inclusion of it in this book. The following persons gave permission to publish quotations: General Mark H. Galusha, General Donald W. McGowan, General Williston B. Palmer, General Milton A. Reckord, Mrs. George Rockwell (daughter of the late General John McAuley Palmer), Senator Leverett Saltonstall, Charles Dale Story, John M. Vorys, and General Ellard A. Walsh.

None of these persons is in any way responsible for what I have written, however much he may have contributed to the writing of it. In particular, General Walsh is not responsible for what I have done with his diaries.

Martha Derthick

CONTENTS

THE NATIONAL GUARD IN POLITICS

CHAPTER I ✦ GROUP POWER: THE CASE OF THE NATIONAL GUARD

This is a study of one of the most successful pressure groups in a political system noted for the advantages that it gives pressure groups. The system is the American, and the group is the National Guard, part-time military force of the federal government and the states. My purpose is to analyze the phenomenon of group power through examination of a particular case.[1]

The case is in many respects an unusual one. As a pressure group, the National Guard has several distinctive advantages. First and most important of all, the Guard has a foundation in the Constitution of the United States. It is the militia to which the following constitutional clauses apply:

> The Congress shall have Power . . .
> To provide for calling forth the Militia to execute the Laws of the Union, suppress Insurrections and repel Invasions;
> To provide for organizing, arming, and disciplining the Militia, and for governing such Part of them as may be employed in the Service of the United States, reserving to the States, respectively, the Appointment of the Officers, and the Authority of training the Militia according to the discipline prescribed by Congress. . . .

Thus the Guard is grounded in the country's fundamental law. Second, and following from its constitutional sanction, the Guard has a public, official character. It is not a private claimant upon government; it is part of the government. In recognition of this, the Justice Department does not require the Guard's lobby, the National Guard Association, to register under the Regulation of Lobbying Act, and the NGA is exempted by act of Congress from real property taxes in the District of Columbia. Third, even as a public organization the Guard has unusual advantages on account of its military character. Its purpose, public defense, endows its claims on public resources with special force. Fourth, the Guard is a nationwide institution, rooted in the city, the village, and rural areas. In 1960 the Army Guard had units in 2534 communities, scattered among forty-nine states and nearly all of the congressional districts. The geographic dispersion of the Guard enhances its access to congressmen; its character as a community institution enhances its appeal to them. Fifth, the Guard is highly organized. As a military organization, it has had a highly regularized system for recruiting members, selecting leaders, and enforcing internal discipline. This has facilitated the concerting of activity by Guard members for political purposes. Few other pressure groups are endowed with so stable an internal structure. Finally, as a result of its connection with state governments the Guard has connections with state party organizations. Historically, the Guard has been a source of patronage for the governors, though not for members of Congress. Many Guard officers have engaged in partisan activity, pursuing careers in politics and the Guard simultaneously. Some have become governors and congressmen. In each state there is an adjutant general, an appointee of the governor (except in Vermont, where he is elected by the legislature, and South Carolina, where he is popularly elected), who is the archetype of the political Guardsman. The adjutant general serves as chief of staff to the governor, administers the state military establishment, and in some cases has command over the Guard, although in many states this authority is reserved to officers of the line.[2] The adjutant general also makes it his business to know the congressmen from his state. The activity of Guardsmen in politics has enhanced their rapport with members of Congress.

For all of these reasons, the Guard cannot be considered a typical pressure group, if there can be a typical member of a universe so varied as that of American pressure groups. Its value as a subject of study lies in the circumstance that it is an unusually successful group. In general, the Guard has gotten what it wanted from government. As an extreme case, it is useful for analyzing the concept of group power.

Since 1879, when the National Guard Association was formed, the Guard has pursued two principal political goals: to secure federal assistance and a role as a front-line reserve to the Regular Army; and to retain legal status as a state military force in peacetime, which gives the Guard freedom from federal control. The Guard has, in other words, called upon Congress to act on behalf of a strong militia. The militia clause might have been allowed to atrophy. Congress might have chosen to organize reserve forces entirely under the clause which gives it power "To raise and support armies." The Guard has argued for vigorous exercise of power under the militia clause.

Evidence of the Guard's success is sown throughout the country—in armories at crossroads towns, in jeeps parked outside county courthouses and state capitols, in jet fighters on the fringes of commercial airports, in uniformed ranks marching down Main Streets on the Fourth of July. As of 1963 there were 380,000 men in the Army National Guard and 70,000 in the Air National Guard. They were recruited under federal statutes, paid with federal money, equipped with material procured by the federal government, and housed in armories for which the federal government had paid much of the construction costs. Federal statutes provide that "In accordance with the traditional military policy of the United States, it is essential that the strength and organization of the Army National Guard and the Air National Guard as an integral part of the first line defenses of the United States be maintained and assured at all times." [3] Still, the Guard continues to serve as a state force in peacetime. It is under command of the governors and available for their use in case of domestic emergency.

The Guard as a whole does not constitute a pressure group.

For political purposes, "the Guard" consists of the men of officer rank. The National Guard Association is an organization of officers; enlisted men are not admitted to membership. Among the officers, the adjutants general have been the most active in asserting the Guard's political interests, especially its interest in freedom from federal control. They have usually dominated the NGA.

Guard officers traditionally have had a passionate devotion to their organization. They have been drawn to the Guard by a desire for military service and the satisfactions associated with it—prestige of uniform and rank, involvement in a cause, excitement and a role to play in times of crises. Many have joined as young men and remained in the Guard all their lives, rising through the ranks. In some families Guard service is a tradition that has been passed down from father to son.[4]

For some men the Guard has been a career. These are the officers, led by the adjutants general, who serve full-time on state staffs. Most Guardsmen, however, have been part-time soldiers. They are civilians but put on uniforms to drill with the Guard on nights, weekends, and at summer camp. The Guard has not been a minor pastime for its members. Even for those— the vast majority—who have not made a career of it, the Guard has been a sustained activity, central to their lives, absorbing much of their time, and commanding deep devotion. While others may have scorned them as pork-barrel politicians, they have prided themselves on their asceticism. "There are no self-seekers in the National Guard," in the words of the most devoted of NGA presidents.[5]

A commission has provided prestige not only within the hierarchy of the Guard but also within the local community—the village, town, or city—of which the officer is a member. Many top-ranking Guard officers have been prominent in their civil capacities, as professional men or business executives. For such men, membership in the Guard has been just one of many

distinctions. But some observers feel that the Guard has also
attracted men who, having in some degree failed in private
life, seek alternative satisfactions in it. There they are endowed
with the authority of rank and the prestige of the uniform of a
United States Army officer.

The satisfactions of Guard membership have not been available to them from any other source. Even if they were attracted
to careers in the Army, a sizable though declining proportion
could not qualify for ranks as high as those they hold in the
Guard. The Guard has traditionally been organized in the same
manner as the Army, in combat units up through division size.
This means that Guard officers can reach the rank held by a
division commander, major general. In the Army, West Point
graduates predominate in such commands as well as many lower
ones. In any case, many Guard officers have not wanted to cut
their community ties for the rootless life of the military professional. The Guard has enabled them to share in both the civilian
and military worlds.*

The Guard has meant different things to different men in
different places (some units, for example, have been socially
more prestigious than others); to all it has meant a great deal.
If the federal government did not recognize the Guard as a
combat organization, if the federal government did not provide
uniforms and equipment, if the federal government rather than
the states controlled the appointment of Guard officers, then the
organization as they know it would cease to exist and the satisfactions of Guard membership would be denied them. That is
why they have joined in political activity.

---

* Since the end of World War I, there has been a federal reserve organization, the Organized Reserves, with an officer component, the Officers'
Reserve Corps, which potentially offers some of the same rewards as a
commission in the Guard. However, only since World War II have enlisted
men been enrolled in the Organized Reserves, making possible the formation of combat divisions. Furthermore, the federal reserve organization is
more closely supervised by the Army, and it lacks the tight-knit quality and
esprit of the Guard.

This book analyzes the political activity of the Guard at the federal level. In concentrating on the political role of the Guard, the analysis ignores its military role. The only battles under study here are political ones. The Guard's combat performance is relevant to its political history. The traditional hostility of the Army to the Guard undoubtedly stems in part (but only in part) from the Guard's shortcomings as a fighting force. Whether the political victories of the Guard are regarded as fortunate or not depends on a judgment of whether the Guard has value as a combat organization. This book makes no assumptions and draws no conclusions with respect to its military value. To do this objectively would require extensive research into combat records and more analysis of military history than is convenient.

By the turn of the century, the militia lobby was known in Washington as a hard one to defeat. Today the Guard is not so well known nationally as it was in more peaceful times, before the professional services achieved their present size and stature, but the NGA's reputation of power survives in the capital. The Guard is often said to be the most powerful of all the military pressure groups. That it "has power" in some sense is very plain. But what sense? That is, what sense of the term "power" will be most useful in describing and explaining the outcomes of the Guard's participation in politics?

THE CONCEPT OF POWER

Political scientists have in recent years spent considerable effort to arrive at a concept of power that will have analytical precision. They have made much progress and experienced much frustration. "Power," in Dahl's definition, which is both representative and lucid, is an actor's (A's) ability to get another actor (B) to do something that B would not otherwise do.[6] A has a *base* of power (resources) and *means* of power (instruments by which he brings his resources to bear on B). He has an *amount* of power (which Dahl represents as a probability that A can get B to act as he otherwise would not). Finally, A's power has *scope* (the range of B's responses). The concept, as Dahl points out, encounters numerous and serious difficulties when an attempt is made to apply it in empirical research. A fundamental difficulty is that of proving that B would not have done what A wanted him to do even in the absence of A's efforts to exert power. Although we can discover that A wanted B to take a certain action, and we can observe that A has certain resources of potential power and used the available means to bring them to bear on B, and we can observe that B took the action that A intended, we still cannot be sure that B would not have taken the action without A's efforts. At least, we would have great difficulty in estimating a probability that A's action affected B, which is what Dahl's conceptual scheme requires if we are to judge the amount of A's power. A further and probably more serious difficulty is that the concept is not useful for comparative purposes. "For the important question is whether we can specify some properties that will insure comparability among actors, respondents, means, and scopes. The answer, alas, is no." [7]

The case of the Guard illustrates well the difficulties of applying this particular concept of power to the situation of an actual pressure group. The National Guard, anyone would agree, "has power"—seemingly a great deal of it—yet it is very difficult to isolate instances when the Guard has gotten Congress, which is its principal object of influence, to do something that Congress would not otherwise have done. Indeed, those actions of Congress that represent the most important "victories" for the Guard are the ones least plainly attributable to the Guard's "power." Factors other than the Guard's attempts to exercise power—such as efforts of its political allies, the predispositions of congressmen, and "circumstances of the moment" arising independently of either Congress or the Guard—go farther toward accounting for Congress' actions on behalf of the Guard than do the Guard's own efforts at inducing the appropriate congressional actions. And if this is true in the case of the Guard, which seems to have important resources of power as well as the means (a lobby) for bringing them to bear on Congress, it must be equally or more true of other so-called "pressure groups" that lack some or all of the Guard's inherent advantages.

A somewhat different concept of power fits the Guard's experience better, and perhaps that of pressure groups in general. "Power" may be thought of as a function of success in realizing "goals." A group is "powerful" or "has power" to the extent that it gets what it wants from government. This approach is different from that of Dahl and most analysts, who begin with a relation between one political actor (the power-holder) and another (the respondent). The extent to which the first "has power" depends on the probability of his affecting the behavior of the other. Here, the starting point is the relation between the goals of an actor and his achievements. A group's power is the ratio of its achievements to its goals. Power is at a maximum when achievements and goals are in balance. Power increases as achievements increase while goals remain constant or as goals decrease while achievements remain constant; it decreases as achievements decrease while goals remain constant or as goals increase while achievements remain constant. (I shall speak of this as a concept of group power, but if it is applicable to the case of a group, it should be applicable as well to political actors other than groups.)

One advantage of this concept is that, by making "power" a function of two variables, it may help to describe the activity of a group over time. A crude hypothesis is that the tendency of group activity over time is to maximize power by keeping goals and achievements in balance. The behavior of the Guard fits this hypothesis fairly well. The concept also facilitates comparisons of the power of the same group at different times.

This concept of power is at least as satisfying to intuition and common sense as any other. In everyday conversation, when we speak of a group or other political actor as "powerful," we seem to mean that it "gets what it wants." The concept satisfies a common-sense need to match achievements against goals in judging power. By defining power as a ratio between achievements and goals, it also forces us to conceive of achievements and goals as having a magnitude, and thereby accords with our ordinary observation (an observation too often overlooked in analyses of group power) that the goals of some groups are "greater" in some sense than those of other groups.

This concept may open new approaches to the problem of the comparability of power. It requires us to consider as equal in power any two groups with the same ratio of achievements to goals. If, say, the Air Force achieves its goals in the same ratio as the National Guard, then we are bound to regard the two as equally powerful. Such a comparison is not without meaning, but it is inadequate and unsatisfying. What we would really want to know is how the Air Force and National Guard compare with repect to the magnitude of their goals and of their achievements. If comparability can be achieved with respect to these magnitudes, then we might have a highly useful concept.

The concept of power proposed here rests on the assumption that "goals" and "achievements" have magnitudes that can be compared. This is plausible as an abstraction. The difficulties arise in achieving definitions of "goals" and "achievements" and in developing criteria for judging their magnitudes such that the concept will be useful in analyzing actual cases. The principal problem is that of defining and measuring goals. If this can be done, achievements can then be judged in relation to them.

Goals. A goal may be defined as a claim communicated to government. That definition will be used in this book. It has one major drawback: it leaves out of account goals that the group desires to achieve but declines to communicate to government on the assumption that they will be denied. It would be desirable to include within "goals" all of the group's interests or needs—all that it really wants or would benefit from having from government—rather than merely what it asks. A group may, according to my definition, claim very little—perhaps much less than it would like to—and still be regarded as powerful as long as it achieves what it claims. On the other hand, this definition of goals is the only one that offers much hope of utility. It is often very difficult for a group, let alone an outside observer, to know what is really in its interest; the observer has little choice except to take the group's express claims upon government as a definitive statement of its goals.

The easiest way to judge the magnitude of a group's goals might at first seem to be by examination of their content. Many claims involve the expenditure of public funds. A claim for $100 million, it might be supposed, is obviously greater than one for $1 million. Other elements of content that would help in assessing magnitude might be isolated. Such an approach presents serious difficulties, of which the most important is that, from the perspective of the government, magnitude is relative. It depends upon the character of the claimant group, and also upon the circumstances in which the claim is advanced. From some groups, a claim for $100 million would seem large; from others, small. Coming from the same group, it might seem large under some circumstances and small under others. Another possibility would be to judge the magnitude of a group's claims according to the importance of the claim to the group itself. Some claims are vital; others, of peripheral interest to the group. This criterion has the disadvantage of leaving the government's views out of account entirely.

Both of these approaches point up a problem of perspective. The most useful conception of magnitude will be one valid from the perspective of both the claimant group and the government, at any point in time and under any circumstances. The conception must take account of the relation between the group and the government; it is this relation that is significant rather than the outlook of either the group or the government in isolation. To conceive of the magnitude of goals as being determined by the degree of resistance to them meets this requirement. Such a conception properly places emphasis on the relation between the group and the government, and it is a conception not limited by time or circumstance.

In order to realize a claim a group must secure the consent of a series of holders of formal authority who may be thought of as constituting a system or potential system of activity. The group encounters such resistance as is associated with the inertia of the system (if the system is viewed as static). If it is assumed instead that the system is normally dynamic, then the group encounters more or less resistance according to whether the tendency of movement is incompatible or compatible with its claims. In either case, the amount of resistance the group encounters is a function of three factors: the number and range of political actors who are involved in processing the claims; the attitudes of these actors; and the existence of competing or supporting claims from related groups.

The number of actors involved in processing a group's claims may be great or small. The more numerous they are, the more resistance the group will encounter, both because it is harder to secure coordination of many actions than a few and because the possible points of opposition are more numerous. The range (or scope) of the system is related to the number of actors in it—the more numerous they are, the greater is the range likely to be—but the term is meant to denote, not a quantity of actors, but the character of the relations among them. The system to which the group must address its claims may consist of actors frequently (and therefore more or less routinely) joined in working relation. They may be closely linked to one another by frequent communications and accustomed to engaging in coordinated action. Or the potential system may be a diffuse, widely dispersed one, composed of a variety of actors who have no or only tenuous working relations with one another. It is possible, for example, for a group active as a claimant upon the federal government to realize a claim of limited interest to others by getting a single congressional committee chairman to promote a bill. Acquiescence is required of a small number of other political actors, including the President, who must sign the bill, but the number of those involved may remain low, and cooperation among them is to a considerable degree routinized. On the other hand, a claim with broad social implications may engage the attention of many congressmen, many executive agencies, the President, and even the public at large. Such a system of political actors is one of wide scope and great complexity within which coordinated action is routinized to but a limited degree. A simple system of narrow range may be stimulated to action with relative ease; a complex one of wide range is a source of potentially much greater resistance.

In addition to the scope and complexity of the system of political actors by which the group's claims are processed, the attitudes of those actors toward the group are a basic determinant of the resistance to its claims. These attitudes may fall anywhere along a continuum ranging from extreme hostility to extreme favor. If they are hostile, resistance may be so great as to make the group's claims impossibly large; if they are extremely favorable, it may be reduced to the minimum that is inescapably associated with stimulating coordinated action in the system.

The third factor that determines the degree of resistance to a group's claims is the incidence and intensity of competing or supporting claims. Supporting claims from allies may help overcome resistance; competing claims from opponents are a source of it. The more numerous and intense are competing claims, the greater resistance is.

How much resistance a particular claim encounters depends

in turn on the content of the claim. A request for a major piece of substantive legislation, with widespread social implications, is bound to engage a wider set of political actors than is, say, a claim for a small additional expenditure of public funds for a purpose already sanctioned. The content of the claim, as well as the character of the claimant group, is a factor of fundamental importance in shaping the attitudes of those actors who must process the claim. For example, a claim that entails low costs to the public generally meets with more favor than one that is costly. Whether a group is faced with a counterclaim depends on whether the content of its own claim infringes the interests of other groups. Some claims do; others do not. The content of a group's claims therefore does affect the degree of resistance the group encounters, but content by itself is an inadequate criterion for judging the magnitude of the group's goals. What is important is how the content is viewed by those to whom the claim is addressed, or whose interests are implicated by it.

Achievements. "Achievements" are actions taken by government in fulfillment of the group's claims. To establish that a group "has power," it is not necessary to judge the extent to which the actions are responses to activities of the group in pursuance of those claims. (This does not mean that it is not desirable to attempt such a judgment, but that the concept of power used here does not depend on the success of the attempt.) An achievement is a goal fulfilled whether or not it can be established that the group "caused" the fulfillment by conscious effort beyond mere assertion of the claim.

The magnitude of a group's achievements may be judged by relating what is achieved to the magnitude of the group's goals. If all claims made are perfectly fulfilled, then the magnitude of the group's achievements equals that of its goals, and its power is at a maximum. To the extent that claims go unfulfilled, the magnitude of achievements falls short of the magnitude of goals (and power is accordingly less).

The Case of the Guard. The Guard has throughout its history been a powerful group. It has generally been able to achieve its principal goals. Its goals have been of low magnitude for several reasons. First, the Guard's claims have rarely implicated a large public. The system of actors to which they have been addressed has ordinarily been simple and restricted. Second, the political actors with authority over the Guard's claims—members of Congress—have usually been favorably predisposed toward it. Third, the Guard has rarely faced strong competing claims, and sometimes it has been helped by supporting claims from a political ally. The activities of the National Guard Association, the means by which the Guard seeks to exercise power in Dahl's sense, have been crucial to its political success, but only because communication of claims is crucial to realization of them. On those occasions when it has met resistance in Congress, the NGA has not been able to overcome that resistance, but has had to withdraw or modify its claims or wait upon a change of circumstances that would put an end to resistance.

The modern National Guard developed in a period of approximately forty years spanning the turn of the century. In the late 1870's, the Guard (or what was to become the Guard, for there was then no organization by that name) consisted of scattered units of men held together by a shared enthusiasm for military activity. They received almost no federal support, and very little from the state governments. Their status as a reserve to the army of the federal government was in doubt. By the time the United States entered World War I, the Guard had 129,000 members organized and uniformed in the same manner as the Army. It received large amounts of support from both the federal and state governments, including both equipment and pay. In fact and in law, it constituted the Army's reserve.

The principal milestones in this transformation were two acts of Congress—the Militia Act of 1903 and the National Defense Act of 1916. They established the Guard in law as a federal reserve; they remain today the source of much of the federal law that pertains to it. Their passage fulfilled the first and most important political goals of the National Guard.

BIRTH OF A PRESSURE GROUP

As of the late 1870's, all men in the United States between the ages of eighteen and forty-five were obligated to serve in the militia and to arm and equip themselves for that purpose. This obligation had been imposed by the Militia Act of 1792. Only a few took it seriously. The act itself, and the annual militia musters that it required, had become a national joke. Within a dozen years after the Civil War, however, increasing numbers of men began to take an interest in the militia. They formed units, drilled, and bought uniforms and arms. They were the nucleus of the National Guard. Very early they turned to political activity.

The National Guard Association was formed to seek a new militia act from Congress. This was to be a major piece of federal legislation to supersede the obsolete act of 1792. The object was to have the Guard recognized in federal law as the "organized militia." This would distinguish Guard members from the vast majority of men between eighteen and forty-five years who were legally classified as militia but who did not actually serve—that is, were "unorganized." The Guard, which was the militia in fact, would be acknowledged as such in law. Not until 1903 was the Guard able to achieve this, its first major political goal. In the meantime, it thrived with help from the states.

Between 1881 and 1892 every state in the Union revised its military code to establish an organized militia, which in almost all of the states was officially named the "National Guard." Many states also provided uniforms, armories, and camp sites. In 1896 state military appropriations totaled $2,799,549. With more than 100,000 officers and men, the Guard was four times the size of the Army. Whether it would supplant the Army was seriously discussed in periodicals.[1]

Both observers in the 1880's and subsequent students have identified the labor riots of 1877 as the cause of the Guard's sudden growth.[2] Unquestionably, industrial violence provided much of the impetus. Fear of violence by "anarchists, internationalists, and nihilists" led state and local governments to strengthen the militia forces.[3] Development of the Guard began and proceeded fastest in the populous, industrial states of the North—Massachusetts, Connecticut, New York, Pennsylvania, Ohio, and Illinois. In addition to appropriations from state and local governments, the Guard received substantial private funds from wealthy businessmen. An Illinois colonel told the NGA convention in 1881:

We have a battalion of five companies of cavalry, all located in the City of Chicago. It grew out of our riots of 1877, previous to which time we had no cavalry in the State. During the riots it was found necessary to have cavalry, and we hastily organized a battalion of cavalry among our business men who had seen cavalry service during the war. Our cavalry was not equipped by the State. It belongs to the National Guard, but was equipped and uniformed complete by the Citizens' Association of the City of Chicago. This association is composed of business men, who look after the best interests of our city.[4]

Officers of the Guard in all of the states appear to have been business and professional men, representative of the "better classes."

It would be a mistake to attribute growth of the Guard entirely to the interest of business groups and state governments in preservation of domestic order. The Guard movement actually got under way even before the labor riots of 1877. Late in 1876 the *Army and Navy Journal* noted that the militia was being transformed in Pennsylvania, New York, and Massachusetts. Massachusetts had "set apart a noble camping ground, with suitable buildings thereon," which, the *Journal* added with a note of approving satire, "like everything else in New England, . . . is intended for use rather than ornament."[5] A variety of factors other than industrial strife contributed to this development.

A good deal of spontaneous martial enthusiasm helped to swell Guard units in the post-Civil War era. There had always been enough amateur military enthusiasts to maintain active volunteer companies in many states, but their number suddenly increased in the 1870's and 1880's. One possible explanation is that many Civil War veterans retained a longing for military association; many Guard officers were veterans, and the leaders of the movement were mostly veterans who held state office as adjutants general or inspectors general.

Walter Millis, noting a "military revival" in this period, suggests that it resulted from the fading of Civil War memories and a consequent tendency to romanticize war.[6] Whatever its source, an element of romanticism was certainly characteristic among leaders of the National Guard. "We rest our faith on cardinal principles," declared the *National Guardsman*, a weekly that began publication in New York in August 1877:

WE BELIEVE IN THE NATIONAL GUARD—in its Divine authentication, its present purpose, and the glorious possibilities of its future. . . .

WE BELIEVE IN RIFLE PRACTICE as an important element of National Guard education—its benefits in promoting manliness, healthfulness, self-reliance, coolness, nerve and skill . . .

WE BELIEVE IN EFFICIENCY on the part of the commissioned officers—that the day has gone by when good-fellowship, a plethoric pocketbook, or political influence could command a commission.

WE BELIEVE IN THE MORAL INFLUENCE FOR GOOD of the citizen soldiery—that the armory and the parade ground, so far from constituting places of contamination, comprehend schools wherein the members of the National Guard may learn their duty to God and man.

Essentially the same values were exalted in less solemn fashion by a pamphlet published in 1884 and called "Joining the Militia, or the Comic Adventures of a Recruit." The hero starts out effeminate and slothful, a militia volunteer for the purpose of evading jury duty. (This was no joke; avoidance of jury duty was a major incentive for many Guard recruits.)[7] After enduring the miseries of a neophyte, the hero begins to realize the benefits of his new life: "He felt active, buoyant and vigorous, and one evening coming from his bath tub he discovered little ridges of muscle rising on his forearm and stretching away toward the shoulder." In the end, he goes to war and gets his woman.

Manliness, physical fitness, duty, and discipline—these were the values that the National Guard promised to serve. It was a fraternal group that fostered loyalty, a social group that promised prestige, an athletic club that promoted physical vigor, and a military organization that offered an opportunity for service. Growth of the Guard may have begun in the urban, industrial North not simply because that was where strikes occurred but also because the Guard met certain social needs of the growing group of office and factory workers there. Most Guard enlisted men were drawn from this group. According to a report on the New Jersey Guard in 1896, the occupational distribution of the members was approximately as follows: merchants or independent business, 13 percent; manufacturing and mechanical industries, 41 percent; clerks, bookkeepers, and so on, 26 percent; salesmen, 9 percent; engineers and railway employees, 8 percent; agriculture, 3 percent. The regimental and company officers were principally independent businessmen or clerks and bookkeepers.[8] For such men, many of whom were newly congregated in cities, the Guard could provide a means of physical recreation and fraternal association.

Newspaper accounts of the Guard stressed its social rather than military functions. The *Springfield Republican*, noted for thorough coverage of the Massachusetts legislature, barely mentioned that state's militia reform bill when it was introduced in 1887. But the paper carried long accounts of a nationwide militia drill contest in Washington and a drill of Massachusetts companies on governor's day at the state militia camp in Framingham. The Chicago company, having scaled a twelve-foot fence, was singled out for praise in the Washington dispatch: "At the word they broke for the fence, rapidly formed a pyramid, tossed up and passed over their guns, and with cat-like agility followed themselves."[9] A widespread fancy for this type of frolic contributed to the Guard's growth along with the more serious purpose of the preservers of public order.

The Guard movement had roots also in nationalism. The birth of the Guard—indeed, the adoption of its very name—was one manifestation of the new forces of national sentiment that were stirring the country.[10] Describing this phenomenon, Arthur M. Schlesinger noted the "Vesuvian energy" that went into the formation of a variety of voluntary nationwide organizations in this period.[11] The National Guard Association was one of these.

Officers who shared an interest in strengthening the Guard met in Richmond in 1878, again in New York in January 1879, and for a third time in St. Louis in October 1879. The NGA was founded at the third meeting with two purposes: "to promote military efficiency throughout the active militia of the United States, and to secure united representation before Congress for such legislation as . . . may [be] necessary for this purpose." [12] The Association submitted a militia reform bill to Congress the following year.

The NGA was not notably successful in its first years. Being new, it was not well organized. It had no paid, permanent lobbyist in Washington, nor did it have an office. Its only funds were the $15 fees collected from each state delegation at conventions. In pursuit of the Guard's political goals, NGA officers petitioned Congress or visited congressmen personally, sometimes at their own expense. The president of the NGA, General George W. Wingate of New York, was especially active in this respect. So was General Albert M. Ordway, commander of the District of Columbia National Guard. The Association as a whole was defunct much of the time. After a convention in 1891 it collapsed altogether for six years. When Guard officers met in St. Louis in 1897, one of the delegates complained: "There is an association called the U. S. National Guard, which is conspicuous for what it doesn't do. The last meeting was in Washington in 1891. We accomplished nothing about as thoroughly as anything you ever saw in your life." [13]

Nonetheless, the political difficulties of the Guard seem to have been more external than internal. Congress simply was not interested in militia reform. This was an era of peace and international isolation for the United States. In the absence of a manifest military danger, Congress was indifferent to military affairs. "What," asked an Iowa representative during debate on a militia bill in 1886, "is the necessity of having any fighting men now?" Representative Forney of Alabama, who was sponsoring the bill, replied, " 'In time of peace prepare for war'; that is the only reason I know. [Laughter]." [14]

Militia legislation was not just laughed off, however. It also encountered explicit opposition from defenders of states' rights, who objected to any new federal action regulating the militia. In 1893 Southern opposition kept a militia reform bill from coming to a vote in the House. A representative from Tennessee complained: "It has got to be a common idea that the people will go to wreck and ruin unless you 'nationalize' everything in which they are concerned." [15]

It was no help to the Guard that the War Department strongly supported its proposal for a new militia act. Beginning in 1878, the chief of ordnance, adjutant general, and secretary of war year after year recommended that Congress increase federal assistance to the Guard. While the NGA was defunct in the early 1890's, Adjutant General J. C. Kelton promoted a militia reform bill. President Benjamin Harrison in 1890 and President Grover Cleveland in 1896 both included these recommendations in their State of the Union messages. [16] The War Department's interest in militia reform seems actually to have increased congressional suspicion of the idea. A representative from New Jersey attacked the bill in 1894 on the grounds that it was backed by "the military organization of this city [which] means to saddle one of its members upon each State in this Union." [17]

The combination of apathy, devotion to states' rights, and antimilitarism prevented the Guard from coming close to success with a reform bill. The Guard did succeed nonetheless with a less ambitious piece of legislation—one that did not propose major innovation, but modified established practice. This was a bill that provided the Guard with increased federal financial support. Since 1808 the militia had been entitled to $200,000 in federal assistance for firearms. The NGA wanted this amount to be increased, and at first combined a proposal for larger appropriations with the bill for militia reform. In the middle eighties, when it became apparent that a reform act would be difficult to pass, the NGA divorced the request for added appropriations from the more controversial parent bill. The wisdom of this tactic was demonstrated in 1887 when Congress authorized annual expenditures of $400,000 for the militia, twice the figure that was fixed in 1808. The *Army and Navy Journal,* pleased with the Guard's success, thought that the secret of the NGA's strength was that "its members did not confine themselves to Congressional lobbying, but were able, through the National Guard of the various States, to bring a personal and direct pressure to bear upon the various Congressmen from their constituents." [18] NGA officers felt that their success in 1887 resulted from having held a convention in Washington in 1885, and consequently they planned to meet in the capital again in 1890. Nothing followed from that convention.

THE MILITIA ACT OF 1903

The Spanish-American War, by suddenly changing the attitude of Congress toward military legislation, paved the way for militia reform. The war dispelled the skepticism of those who doubted that the United States would ever fight. It demonstrated the need for a trained reserve by exposing the inadequacies of the militia, who, as volunteers for federal service, reported to their training camps pathetically ill-prepared. It suffused the country with a martial spirit, and it greatly accelerated the development of nationalism, thereby reducing states'-rights opposition to a federal militia act.[19]

Despite all this, the NGA was not able to get a reform act passed. Once again it got Congress to increase appropriations for the Guard ($1 million annually was authorized in 1900), but militia reform was for the moment more than the Guard could achieve. The difficulty this time was not that such an act seemed to Congress unnecessary or too novel. Instead, Guard members could not agree on what they wanted. The NGA, having been revived at St. Louis in 1897, was no more tightly knit than before. It could not define the Guard's goals with enough precision to make a convincing case before Congress.

The men who revived the NGA in 1897 were almost entirely from Midwestern and Southern states. In this group were the Guard's militants, hostile to the Army and determined in defense of states' rights. As evidence of their emphasis on state interests in the Guard, they called the revived organization the "Interstate National Guard Association." * Confronted with the problem of militia reform after the turn of the century, they favored giving the Guard the largest possible wartime role. They wanted it to fight as long as possible wherever possible, inside or outside of the country. In 1898, on the eve of the war, this group succeeded in getting Congress to emasculate a War Department bill that would have substantially increased the Army and provided that officers for this enlarged force would be commissioned from within the regular corps on the basis of seniority. National Guardsmen who claimed that the bill would ruin the militia and rob them of commissions found numerous congressional champions.[20]

An Eastern group in the Guard, centered in New York State— which had the biggest and best-financed Guard in the country —took a different attitude toward militia reform. This group favored a restricted wartime role for the Guard. In their view it should serve as a stopgap force, returning to office and armory as soon as volunteers were ready. In this group, which was nationalistic rather than localistic in orientation, there was strong sentiment for either turning the Guard over to the federal government or creating a wholly new federal reserve. Under such a proposal, the militia clause of the Constitution would have been ignored, and reserve forces would have been established under

*This name continued in use until World War I. However, for the sake of consistency, the name of the Association will be abbreviated throughout as NGA.

the army clause. Members of this group were embarrassed by the opposition of Midwestern Guardsmen to increasing the Army in 1898.[21]

There is no solid evidence to explain the sources of this schism, but quite probably it grew out of differing interests in the Guard rather than differing philosophies with respect to division of federal and state power or differing tastes for participation in combat. Leading Guard officers in New York were professional men, often lawyers, of considerable wealth and social standing. For them the Guard was not a source of livelihood; it was a fashionable way of demonstrating their patriotism. They did not want to leave their law offices for long months in combat. The leaders of the Guard in the Midwest and South, by contrast, appear to have been adjutants general and other full-time state officers for whom the Guard was the principal source of livelihood, or they were business and professional men of modest accomplishment for whom the Guard was a crucially important source of social prestige. The Guard meant more to them than to the leading officers in New York.* Whatever its source, this division prevented the Guard from taking the initiative toward militia reform. At the meeting in 1897 the NGA did not even show interest in a reform bill, preferring to concentrate on an increase in federal appropriations. It was left to Secretary of War Elihu Root to draft a militia reform act and shepherd it through Congress.

Root would undoubtedly have preferred creating a new, wholly federal reserve to reforming the Guard for federal purposes, but it was clear in 1900 that this idea was too novel to be accepted by Congress, just as a few years earlier militia reform had seemed too novel. Besides, the political success of National Guard officers in 1898 had indicated that even though the Guard could not unite on a positive goal, a faction could

---

* This hypothesis might be tested by historical research into selected state Guard organizations.

prevent legislation that it considered harmful.[22] The debate then had demonstrated Congress' attachment to the Guard. When confronted with the necessity of passing military legislation, Congress had favored the Guard at the expense of the Army. Its preference rested partly on the dogma that standing armies endanger liberty. Congressmen had also argued that a citizen militia served the cause of patriotism. Militiamen, with roots in local communities, would return to their homes after the war and be living symbols of national service; professional soldiers would be isolated in army camps. Citizen-soldiers under federal control would have had these same virtues, but the Guard, with its foundation in the militia clause, served the interest of the states and had a headstart on a federal reserve. It was an established organization which Congress could be expected to protect on grounds of interest (both Congress' and the Guard's) as well as constitutional dogma. Therefore, rather than attempt creation of a federal reserve in lieu of the Guard, the War Department continued to pursue the goal of militia reform that it had set well before the war.

Root bore the burden not only of persuading the Congress to pass a bill, but also of persuading the factions of the Guard to agree on one. In order to compromise the basic issue within the Guard, Root proposed that the militia should be subject to a call for nine months' federal service. This appears to have been too little to satisfy the Midwestern wing of the Guard and too much for the New Yorkers, but it was a provision on which both could agree. Root won the support of Guard officers for his bill at a meeting at his home in Washington in 1902. A convention of the NGA then approved it and Root had it introduced in Congress. Thereafter he carefully cultivated support for the bill among congressmen and newspaper editors, and fended off amendments from the Guard and from Congress that might have upset the compromise.[23]

Congress passed the bill with little controversy, except over authorization of a 100,000-man volunteer federal reserve to serve as a third line behind the Guard. Root, the author of the provision, was eager to have it adopted, and it had been agreed to by the leaders of the NGA. It was included in the bill passed by the House, but encountered Southern opposition in the Senate. Believers in states' rights who earlier had opposed militia reform were now ready to accept that, but not a federal reserve even if it were to be of inferior standing to the Guard. Root sacrificed the federal reserve provision in order to achieve militia reform.[24]

The Militia Act bore the name of General Charles F. Dick, who was chairman of the Militia Committee in the House, president of the NGA, and commanding general of the Ohio National Guard. National Guardsmen have canonized him as the father of the modern Guard. Besides being chairman of the Militia Committee, Dick had party ties that suggest that he could have had more than ordinary influence in Congress and hence could have played a major role in passage of the act. An aide to William McKinley and Mark Hanna, Dick headed eight electoral campaigns in Ohio as chairman of the state Republican executive committee. During the Spanish-American War he was a lieutenant colonel in the Eighth Ohio Regiment—"McKinley's Own"—and secretary of the Republican National Committee. In 1898 he was elected to Congress from Ohio's 19th District, which once had been James A. Garfield's, and three years later, although he lacked seniority, he became chairman of the Militia Committee.* Unfortunately, there is no documentary evidence on Dick's role in passage of the Militia Act. There is almost nothing about the act in his papers, which show him, at least

* There may be no significance in Dick's rapid rise to the position of committee chairman. The practice of filling chairmanships according to seniority was not so strictly adhered to in his day as it is now. According to Joseph Cooper, "prior to 1919 [seniority] had never been allowed to be all-determining in fact or treated as inviolable in theory." It had been only "an important factor in appointment." ("Congress and Its Committees: A Historical and Theoretical Approach to the Proper Role of Committees in the Legislative Process," unpub. diss. Harvard, 1960, p. 157).

in party affairs, to have been a follower of others (McKinley and Hanna) rather than a man of independent influence. Dick's interest in the bill undoubtedly facilitated its movement through Congress, yet the evidence is conclusive that it was Root's initiative that gave impetus to the "Dick" Act. Root knew Dick only formally, and their cooperation on the act appears to have been slight.[25]

AFTERMATH OF MILITIA REFORM

There is no evidence that Guardsmen felt they had sacrificed anything of importance in order to gain their goal of federal recognition and support. The NGA convention in May, 1903, first after militia reform was enacted, gave Root a huge ovation. "The National Guard never had a better friend than Secretary Root," General Dick, as NGA president, said in introducing him. Yet the Militia Act of 1903, besides establishing the Guard clearly in law as a reserve to the Army and authorizing federal uniforms and equipment, also subjected it to substantial federal control. The law prescribed that within five years the organization, armament, and discipline of the militia should conform to that of the Army. Twenty-four armory drills and one five-day encampment a year were required of each state Guard to qualify for federal assistance. The Guard was made liable to nine months' service for the purposes prescribed in the Constitution (repel invasions, suppress insurrections, execute the laws of the Union).[26] These provisions meant that the Guard would require more of the members' time and serious attention.

Not many Guardsmen in 1903 were conscious of the potential consequences of these changes, or if they were, they were not concerned, so pleased were they with passage of the act. The Guard had at this time only a vague, partially formed conception of its interests. Acquisition of federal assistance was an overriding goal. The possible costs of such assistance seem to have been ignored. Within five years after militia reform had been passed, the NGA and the War Department cooperated in amending the act to strengthen still further the Guard's role as a federal reserve force and increase federal assistance to it. The Militia Act of 1908 removed some of the compromises of the earlier act. Whereas in 1903 it had been specified that the Guard might serve only in the United States and for no longer than nine months, the amendments of 1908 provided that it could serve either inside or outside the country for any period the President might specify. Guardsmen were no longer required to undergo a medical examination after being called forth by the President, but were to be mustered without further enlistment or medical examination. Congress authorized an additional $2 million a year in federal funds, which, with the $1 million authorized in 1900 and another $1 million authorized in 1906, brought the annual total for the Guard to $4 million. The act of 1908 also provided that the Guard should be called into service in advance of a volunteer army. Here was absolute assurance of a place at the front, right behind the Army.[27] Congressional opponents of the act argued that, in asking for it, the Guard was ignorant of its effects. Desirous simply of more money, the Guard would be drawn unwittingly under professional control. Seventy-nine members of the House voted against the bill, 126 for it. Passage, the next NGA convention was frankly told, had been "a difficult matter." The NGA executive committee chairman advised Guard officers to wait before placing further demands upon Congress, especially if they involved additional appropriations.[28]

The militia acts of 1903 and 1908 had considerable impact on the Guard. Many men who were in the Guard largely for fun or because it was fashionable seem to have left the organization in succeeding years. Leadership of the NGA passed securely to men who sought a combat role for the Guard. Some members in New York continued to have reservations about the Guard's development as a combat force, but their voice was muffled, their influence declining.

Although social benefits, such as the use of the armory as a club, continued to be important incentives to membership, it was clear by 1909 that the sheer love of martial association was not sufficient to sustain the Guard. The demands imposed by the militia acts with respect to federal service and training time were causing some men to leave the Guard and those who stayed to seek compensation. In 1910 the NGA began to demand federal pay for armory drills.[29] This was a major political goal, comparable in importance to the earlier goal of a militia reform act. It was achieved in 1916 with passage of the National Defense Act, but only after a bitter struggle with the War Department, which ceased in the early 1900's to be the Guard's staunch political ally and instead became its political enemy.

THE CAMPAIGN FOR DRILL PAY

The Guard's campaign for armory drill pay, like its earlier campaign for militia reform, failed at first, but for different reasons. War Department opposition this time was the chief obstacle to success. The NGA could not get Congress to pass a bill unless the War Department would approve, and the War Department demanded stronger measures of control over the Guard than either the Guard or Congress would agree to.

The War Department's attitude toward the Guard changed radically as the twentieth century moved into its second decade. This was the result of changes within the War Department over which the Guard had not the slightest control. In the years before World War I, leading officials of the Department, both military and civilian, were imbued with a spirit of nationalism and a desire for efficiency which led them to concentrate authority at the recently created apex of Army administration—the General Staff. Among the men prominently associated with this movement—besides Root, who started it—were General Leonard Wood, chief of staff from 1910 to 1914, Henry L. Stimson, secretary of war from 1911 to 1913, and Lindley M. Garrison, secretary of war from 1913 to 1916. These men sought to abolish small Army posts and concentrate troops in efficient tactical units, to develop a comprehensive policy for the Army, and to end piecemeal legislation by appropriations riders. Above all, they sought to improve the reserve forces, either by creating a new, wholly federal reserve or by increasing the control of the General Staff over the organization and training of the National Guard.[30]

The Guard was prominent among the obstacles in the way of these reformers of national military policy. Inherently resistant to central control, it was bound to confound their purposes, though they had difficulty accepting this fact. From 1910, when Wood became chief of staff, until 1916, when the issues of military policy came before Congress for resolution, the Guard and the War Department were constantly at odds.

They fought over a Department circular of 1913 that restricted the number of staff officers attached to Guard units. The political leadership and influence of the National Guard lay in large part with these men. The adjutants general, subordinate staff members, and unit commanders at the top of the state military organizations were the most active members of the NGA. Occasionally their personal interests could be perceived in NGA positions on federal legislation, noticeably in resistance to the War Department's demand that the President appoint the chiefs of staff and assistant chiefs of staff of Guard divisions and in long-standing insistence that the Guard should enter the federal service in units larger than a regiment. The NGA executive committee chairman told the 1914 convention that, unless the status of the highest-ranking Guard officers could be safeguarded by legislation, "when the time of trouble comes their organizations, if efficient, may be taken but they ... will be left at home to explain to their friends the humiliation they have suffered." [31] There is evidence that the junior officers and enlisted men of the Guard might have preferred to leave their generals at home, but the NGA did not represent the interests of the lower ranks, insofar as they differed from those of the highest ones. [32]

The Guard and the War Department also fought over the Department's efforts to improve surveillance of federal expenditures for the Guard. They fought over whether the Guard should continue to have priority over individual volunteers for service in wartime. They fought over the composition of the Guard, which included some units the Department thought were not necessary and failed to include some the Department thought were. Above all, they fought over the Guard's proposed pay bill.

More than once, agreement on the pay bill seemed likely, but something always prevented a permanent understanding. When the NGA first proposed militia pay in 1910, Chief of Staff Wood warmly endorsed the idea before the NGA convention. Before long, he demanded that the bill include strong new provisions of federal control. Partly on account of these provisions, the bill encountered opposition in the House from antimilitarist congressmen and defenders of states' rights. Another ground for opposition was that the bill would cost too much money. [33] It died in the Senate.

In 1912 the NGA and the War Department agreed on a bill that greatly strengthened federal control over the Guard, and they were about to support it jointly before Congress when the administration of the Department changed following the presidential election. The new secretary, Garrison, objected that federal controls over the Guard should be even more stringent. Lacking support from the War Department, the NGA hesitated to pursue the pay bill. Neither Military Affairs Committee chairman would proceed with a bill until it had been approved by the Administration.

The NGA might have been able to act more effectively if it

had been united, but as in 1903, it could not decide exactly what the Guard's goals should be. The leaders were divided into militants and moderates, the former hostile to the War Department, the latter hopeful of cooperation.[34] This schism did not develop, however, until the drive for drill pay was well advanced. Meanwhile the NGA lobbied hard for the bill and with some effect. On the eve of the 1910–1911 session, the NGA executive committee chairman wrote the adjutants general urging them to seek passage and to report on the attitude of congressional delegations from their states. He was in Washington arranging for introduction of the bill and hearings. A number of adjutants general testified for the bill and all were kept informed of its progress and urged to telegraph their congressmen as a vote approached. When it was necessary to get a special rule from the House Rules Committee in order to permit passage by a simple majority rather than a two-thirds vote, the NGA summoned the adjutant general and other officers from Pennsylvania to approach the chairman, Pennsylvanian John Dalzell. The Guard methodically exploited its resources of influence on the local level. Concentrating on key committee figures or the uncommitted congressman, NGA leaders stimulated pressure from Guard officers in a congressman's own district. They also sought support from Guard enlisted men and influential community leaders, especially businessmen. At their command was a ready-made network of political influence built on military organization and extending into every part of the country. If congressional committee chairmen were Republicans, the burden of persuasion was on Guard officers in the North. When control of Congress switched to the Democrats, the call for help was sounded in the South. The chairman of the NGA executive committee was a political general with a vast chain of command. But his political army was of no avail as long as the War Department opposed it before Congress.[35]

THE NATIONAL DEFENSE ACT OF 1916

Conflict between the Guard and the War Department was seriously joined in the preparedness debate of 1915–16, after World War I began. The war, by opening the way for major innovations in military policy, profoundly altered the setting of the Guard's political activity, as the Spanish-American War had done a dozen or more years before. The War Department, hoping to exploit the fresh impulses of nationalism, sought to create a federal reserve, the continental army, to replace the Guard. President Wilson proposed such a force to Congress in December 1915. The Guard saw an opportunity to realize its long-standing goal of armory drill pay. The principal issue in the preparedness debate, therefore, was this: whether to create a new federal reserve force or continue relying on the Guard and give it greater federal support. Congress resolved this issue in favor of the Guard, but only after the Guard had made far greater concessions to federal control than it had contemplated.

The National Defense Act that was passed in June 1916 reaffirmed the combat reserve role of the Guard, provided it with armory drill pay, and authorized a peacetime strength of 425,000, a three-fold increase. The NGA's reputation as an influential lobby dates in large part from this success, and the Guard's lobbying itself became an issue in the debate of 1916. Nevertheless, the NGA played a limited role in the evolution of the National Defense Act.

Many factors in the Guard's political setting combined to make victory over the War Department likely. The most important of these was the role of Congressman James Hay, chairman of the House Military Affairs Committee. Hay dominated congressional action in military matters, and he was strongly predisposed to favor the Guard—or at least to oppose creation of a federal reserve. A veteran member of the Virginia delegation and son of a Confederate Army surgeon, Hay had for several years been a major antagonist of the War Department's nationalist reformers of military policy. He was particularly suspicious of the General Staff, from which the continental army plan came. Hay was not a pacifist, but he was, in the parlance of the day, a "little Army" man, opposed on principle to aggrandizement of the Army, as were a majority of his committee. He was also an extremely powerful figure. His own succinct view, set forth some years later, was that "I had the confidence of the House, which followed me in all military matters." Jealous of his authority, he resented the remote, righteous man at the head of the War Department, who in 1916 urged the continental army upon Congress. Some time later, Hay recalled that Secretary Garrison "was an able and diligent executive officer, but he at no time, during the incumbency of his office, was in accord with Congress, nor did he seem to think it necessary to consult the chairmen or members of the military committees of the two houses, upon questions of military policy and national defense." [36] Both as a believer in states' rights and as an antagonist of the War Department, Hay was bound to favor the Guard in the debate of 1915–16.

Furthermore, his principal source of advice and help was likewise an opponent of the continental army proposal. This was Major General Fred C. Ainsworth, a man with ample reason to upset the plans of the General Staff. A former adjutant general of the Army, Ainsworth had left the War Department in 1912, under threat of a court martial, following a bureaucratic conflict with Chief of Staff Wood. For Ainsworth, that was the end of a fierce struggle to protect an entrenched staff agency, the Adjutant General's Office, against the centralized supervision of the General Staff. As an enemy of the General Staff, he was a natural ally of the National Guard; there is no reason to suppose that he was under the influence of the National Guard Association.[37]

The Hay bill, foundation of the National Defense Act, was in

large part the work of Hay and Ainsworth. Hay later acknowledged Ainsworth's help with this tribute:

> I cannot fail . . . to give to Major General Fred C. Ainsworth the
> credit, which he deserves, in the preparation and passage of the
> National Defense Act. He was my adviser and helper throughout.
> Without his vast knowledge of military law, his genius for detail, his
> indefatigable industry in preparing the legislation, and meeting the
> numerous arguments which were urged against it, it would not have
> been possible for me to have carried through the legislation. No man
> ever gave his time and labor so generously to any cause, and that too
> with the promise which he exacted from me that he was not to be
> mentioned as my aid and helper.[38]

The bill reflects the joint purpose of Hay and Ainsworth to
circumscribe the authority of the General Staff. As enacted, it
increased the General Staff from 38 to 55 (the General Staff had
asked for 121), but the increase was more than nullified by a
provision that only half of the 55 could be on duty in or near
the District of Columbia. The functions of the General Staff
were newly defined to prohibit duties "of an administrative
nature." Of four divisions that had composed the General Staff,
three (including the Militia Affairs Division) were transferred
from it or abolished.

The value to the Guard of Hay's and Ainsworth's support
would be hard to overestimate. Ironically, the Guard found
support of a kind also from normally hostile sources. The strong-
est advocates of preparedness doubted the practicality of the
continental army. Leonard Wood doubted that the continental
army could be raised from volunteers and advocated instead a
program of universal military training, the very suggestion of
which outraged the antimilitarists in Congress. In addition, the
Guard had the advantage of being in existence, a force of
129,000 men eager to serve the federal government and in turn
be supported by it. This meant that reform of the Guard was
the most practical course.

It was also the most sensible course politically. The Guard

existed as a recognizable interest group, which would be angered by adverse legislation. The continental army, by contrast, was a phantom in the minds of War Department planners. By ignoring the interests of the Guard, the President and Congress stood to make a number of enemies but few friends; by protecting the interests of the Guard, they stood to make a number of friends and few enemies.

Both President Wilson and Congressman Hay were conscious of this. Even before the War Department's plan had been made public, Wilson received a letter from the adjutant general of New Jersey, Wilbur F. Sadler, whom he knew from his days as New Jersey's governor, warning vigorously against adoption of the continental army plan. Sadler wrote to J. P. Tumulty, Wilson's secretary:

Dear Joe: For God's sake don't let the President make the mistake of endorsing the Garrison program for greater land defense. . . . Garrison's program has made the officers and men of the Guard furious and the President, if he endorses the program, will make more determined enemies than you know. . . . If you save him from this course you will be doing him the biggest favor imaginable.[39]

Tumulty showed the letter to Wilson. Shortly after reading it, the President urged upon Garrison the necessity of conserving the "dignity and importance" of the Guard. Hay probably had this in mind when he wrote the President in February recommending a bill based on reform of the Guard:

There are some political considerations to which I think I ought to call your attention. The people in a democracy like ours, must be consulted, and I am within the bounds of reason when I say, that the National Guard plan is favored by a very large majority of the people.[40]

"The people" whom Hay had in mind were probably members of the National Guard. As an established interest it had to be heeded.

Unlike the Guard, the War Department had no public constituency. It had articulate supporters, but they were concentrated in the cities of the east coast—New York and, to a lesser extent, Philadelphia and Boston. By comparison with the Guard, these public leaders of the preparedness movement were a small, geographically confined, and amorphous group.[41]

Another political consideration was that "federalization" of the Guard, as the Hay proposal was called, would prevent a split among the Democrats in Congress, which was important to the President in an election year. Some members of the party were extreme advocates of preparedness; others were extreme antimilitarists. The Guard was a convenient vehicle for compromise. Hay pointed out in his February letter to the President:

. . . how important it is that we should have a plan which will not only unite our own party, but which will bring the opposition to the support of your policies. . . . It will, if you will permit me to say so, be a very great triumph for you, if the entire Congress shall adopt what you propose. Mr. Kitchin [Claude Kitchin of North Carolina, the Democratic majority leader in the House and a foe of preparedness] informed me on Saturday last that he would not oppose the National Guard plan.[42]

Though it meant the sacrifice of his secretary of war (Garrison resigned), Wilson acquiesced in Hay's proposal, taking the position that he would accept any bill that would meet the twin requirements of constitutionality and adequate federal control over the Guard.

Wilson personally studied the draft that Hay and Ainsworth prepared to make sure that it authorized sufficient federal control over the Guard. He got advice from Attorney General Thomas W. Gregory, Secretary of the Treasury William G. McAdoo, and Postmaster General Albert S. Burleson, who regularly functioned as his liaison man with Congress. Throughout preparation of the Hay bill, the War Department was a diffident spectator. The Guard could scarcely have faced a weaker, less effectual opponent. Garrison had gone home to New Jersey, and for a month, until Newton D. Baker arrived from Cleveland early in March to take his place, Chief of Staff Hugh L. Scott acted as secretary of war. A benign, grandfatherly man, renowned as a master of sign language, Scott could communicate with wild men on two sides of the Pacific, but he never penetrated the mystery of the American congressman. Ill at ease in what he called the "guileful city" of Washington, he was no man to wage a fight for the Army's interests. "Don't you think," Wilson at one point inquired of his postmaster general, busily engaged in the making of military policy, "[that] we had better lay a corrected copy of the Bill before General Scott for comment and criticism?" [43]

The Hay bill passed the House in March, 402 to 2, fulfilling almost to perfection Hay's hope for solid backing. It provided 40,000 additional men for the Army besides the more than threefold increase for the Guard. Wilson sent Hay a warm letter of congratulations.

The threat to the Guard had not entirely passed, despite rejection of the continental army by the House. Chairman George Chamberlain of the Senate Military Affairs Committee was highly sympathetic to the General Staff and hopeful of retaining something of its original proposal for a continental army. Chamberlain's bill differed from the Hay bill chiefly in calling for a larger increase in the Army, a smaller increase in the Guard (though it too provided federal pay), and creation of a 261,000-man federal reserve similar to the continental army. Despite efforts by the NGA to have it removed, the provision for a federal reserve was retained by the Senate, but the authorizing language was drastically narrowed in conference. As adopted on June 3, the act was based on the Hay bill, although it provided a greater increase for the Army. The Guard emerged from the preparedness debate with its federal reserve role newly confirmed and its financial support from the federal government greatly enlarged.

ROLE OF THE NATIONAL GUARD ASSOCIATION

Preparedness advocates, employing the hyperbole characteristic of the period, vigorously assailed the NGA for its activity
in 1916. Angered by the Guard's opposition to the federal reserve
provision in his bill, Senator Chamberlain declared on the floor
that if the Guard were to become a "political force," he would
favor eliminating it entirely, "not because I love Caesar less,
but because I love Rome more." Leonard Wood warned against
growth of the Guard lobby in a long memorandum to Colonel
Edwin M. House. To provide the Guard with pay, he predicted,
would make it "solid and effective in only one line, and that will
be in a raid on the federal treasury." To Chief of Staff Scott, it
appeared that Congress had been cowed. He wrote to a friend,
"A man from Ohio was in here not long ago, threatening around,
saying that the National Guard has 80,000 votes in Ohio, and
were going to get their way. . . . There is no doubt about it
that the average Congressman is afraid of them." * Hay in
particular was stigmatized in pro-preparedness newspapers and
magazines as a "pork-barrel politician." 44

There is no way to tell for certain whether or to what extent
Hay was influenced by the NGA, but there is strong evidence
that he was not influenced very much. He was probably no
more an agent of the Guard's lobby in 1916 than Elihu Root was

* A test of the Guard's vote-getting power in Ohio followed very shortly
and did not substantiate the man's claim. General Dick, the alleged father
of militia reform and a former representative and senator from Ohio,
ran for nomination as the Republican candidate for senator in 1916.
In a letter that is preserved in the Scott MSS, General A. B. Critchfield,
who had been adjutant general of Ohio, wrote all Guardsmen in the
state asking them to vote for Dick. Dick finished third in the primary
with 37,183 votes out of 271,994 cast. Of course, not all of the 80,000 votes
claimed for the Guard in Ohio would have been Republican ones; assuming
that half, or 40,000, of them were, and allowing for the votes that Dick
presumably got from other sources, the Guard could not have provided
him with more than a fraction of its alleged potential. The Critchfield
letter was the only concrete evidence that research for this book revealed
of an effort by the Guard to concert its votes.

in 1903. In 1910 he was a leader of the congressional group that objected to a militia pay bill because it would extend federal powers too far. As chairman of the Military Affairs Committee after 1911 he had declined to introduce the pay bill in the House. The chief of the War Department's Division of Militia Affairs, one of the Army's most distinguished generals, described Hay in 1914 as "a strong man [who] does his own thinking and comes to his own conclusions." [45] His whole record in Congress, as well as his Southern origin, presaged his opposition to a federal reserve and preference for the Guard. That the War Department ignored this fact was probably the result of its political naïveté and a misunderstanding. Hay did assure the President in the summer and again in the fall of 1915 that he would support a preparedness program; the War Department apparently accepted this as assurance that he would support the continental army. [46]

NGA officials did not consider Hay to be particularly friendly or responsive. In 1920 one of them recalled with considerable candor: "Mr. Hay was chairman of the committee, and it was his bill, and he was rather hard-headed and hewed strictly to the lines he had in mind, and therefore it was not quite as we thought it should be. But we all felt that the law was a good one." [47] Hay had ignored urgent appeals from the NGA in 1916. The NGA executive committee asked for thirty amendments to his bill, of which two were of especial importance. [48] One of these would have given the Guard representation in the General Staff. Hay rejected this, preferring to remove militia affairs from the General Staff entirely. Another amendment would have required the War Department to accept Guard organizations intact. The bill provided instead that in case of war Guardsmen would be drafted as individuals, thereby sacrificing a principle for which the Guard had long contended.

Despite the outraged rhetoric it inspired, the NGA's lobbying in 1916 was relatively modest. In January the NGA executive committee met in Washington and issued a circular to NGA members calling for defeat of the continental army. Thereafter the chairman of the executive committee and one or two other committee members remained in Washington to watch the progress of the bill, keep other Guard officers informed with mimeographed bulletins, and ask them for telegrams in support of the Guard's position. The NGA's budget, normally around $2000 a year, did not pass $4000 in 1916. The NGA still had no official headquarters and no paid staff.[49]

The NGA tried hard to amend the Chamberlain bill, with but limited success. It failed to have the provision for a federal reserve dropped. It succeeded in adding representation for the Guard on the General Staff, but this provision was lost in the House-Senate conference on the bill. If the Guard lobby appeared especially menacing in 1916, this was partly because the continental army plan had united the Guard in self-defense. Internal conflicts were temporarily repaired for the purpose of opposing this threat, but they recurred when new legislation concerning the Guard was under consideration.

As in 1903, the Guard had only a vague, partially formed conception of its interests. A former NGA executive committee chairman, General Edward C. Young of Illinois, actually opposed the Hay bill because it surrendered a large amount of authority over the Guard to the federal government. Young's spokesman in Congress, Representative Burnett M. Chiperfield, charged that the Hay bill was "absolutely illegal" and "in utter defiance" of the Constitution. He declared, "there has been a surrender by certain officers representing the National Guard ... of the rights belonging to [the] States in order that the advantages conferred upon persons in the National Guard by this bill might be gained."[50] Most Guard officers, however—whatever their earlier views on the issue of federal control—supported the Hay bill with enthusiasm. The adjutant general of Colorado, who in 1913 had been one of the fiercest opponents of War Department control, told Congress, "We yearn with our whole souls for an opportunity to federalize."[51]

This lack of consensus had made it difficult for the Guard to pursue political goals with vigor before the war, but the same lack subsequently facilitated accommodations to increased pressures for federal control. Because the Guard did not have a sharply defined conception of its interests, it was able to adjust to the demands of the moment with relative ease. A capacity to adapt its goals in this way was essential to the Guard's political success in 1916.

The Militia Act of 1903 and the National Defense Act of 1916 remain the outstanding political achievements of the National Guard. They established the Guard as the nation's principal military reserve force. They authorized large amounts of federal support for it without destroying its independent status as a state force in peacetime. They fulfilled the Guard's basic goals.

The reasons for the Guard's success were quite similar in both cases. One was that war created a favorable setting for the Guard. It made Congress receptive to new military legislation. Antimilitarists and defenders of states' rights revised their views under the impact of the nation's involvement, or impending involvement, in military conflict. Another reason was that the Guard did not face strong political opposition. With respect to the Militia Act, it faced no opposition whatever. The War Department acted as an ally, as a consequence of its own interest in creating a reserve force. In 1916 the Department's role was reversed, but its influence was nullified by the naïveté of its position, the lack of effective leadership during much of the debate, and the lack of a public constituency. In both cases the Guard had the advantage of being an established, recognizable interest. To be sure, it was asking new legislation, but in 1903 it was asking Congress only to recognize and regularize a *de facto* situation. With support from the states, the Guard had developed into the acknowledged reserve force of the Army, however hazy its legal status may have been. In 1916 its goals were clearly defensive as well as offensive. Whereas the War Department was proposing creation of an entirely new reserve force, the Guard was simply proposing self-perpetuation and enhancement. Assuming that, in both cases, *some* new reserve forces legislation was to be passed, the choice facing Congress was either to ignore the Guard, an established, recognizable interest, or to build upon it. Choosing the latter course did not involve damaging the interests of any other identifiable group of congressional constituents. In 1916 it meant ignoring the War Department bureaucracy, but congressmen (or at least Hay, the congressman most influential in Guard matters) were inclined to view the Department as a political antagonist in any case. Finally, the Guard served widely shared purposes and values. As a military reserve organization, it served the purpose of national defense. As a citizen military organization with a foundation in the state governments, it also served the symbolic values of states' rights and patriotism on the community level.

In these victories, the Guard's lobby played two roles. First, it performed the basic function of formulating the Guard's positive claims and communicating them to Congress. The idea of a militia reform act originated with the NGA. So did the idea of federal pay for the Guard in combination with increased federal control over it. By advancing these proposals to Congress repeatedly, the NGA made them cease to seem novel. When war created pressure for new military legislation, the NGA's proposals were most acceptable to Congress in part because they were already familiar. Second, the NGA performed the equally basic function of communicating to Congress negative claims—that is, objections to legislation potentially harmful to the Guard. By reminding Congress of the Guard's interests, the NGA could exercise a veto in matters of concern to the Guard. This happened in 1898, when objections from the Guard prevented an increase in the Regular Army. It may have happened in 1916, when objections from the Guard were one factor in Congress' rejection of the continental army. Whether or not they were the most important factor is impossible to say. Opposition to the continental army was too varied and too firmly grounded in common sense to permit singling out the NGA's activity as crucial.

The Guard's capacity to voice claims through its lobby was essential to political success. Nevertheless, it is important to recognize the limits of the NGA's effectiveness. Until war created a favorable setting, the NGA was unable to achieve either of its major goals. It was able to make limited gains, such as increases in appropriations, and these increased the substance of the organization and set precedents for further action in its favor. Yet they fell short of what the Guard most wanted.

There were several reasons for the NGA's inability to achieve more. One was congressional reluctance to compromise states' rights. Another was congressional reluctance to make substantial increases in federal expenditure for military purposes in the absence of clear need. A very important reason, in the case of militia pay, was the opposition of the War Department. In both cases, the NGA's inability to unite on specific goals was a reason. The NGA could formulate the Guard's position in only the most general way, and even then there were dissenters. Dissension within the Guard might have fatally undermined the Guard's case in 1903 and 1916 except that Congress was under considerable pressure both times to take action. This meant that the NGA need only block off alternatives unfavorable to the Guard. This it could do despite internal conflicts over positive goals.

CHAPTER III ✦ YEARS OF

STABILITY: 1920–1945

The years from the end of the First World War to the end of the Second were a stable interlude in the Guard's otherwise active political life. These were also transitional years: they are the bridge between the first phase of the Guard's political activity, when its goals were predominantly offensive, to the most recent period, during which it has been defending itself against change.

The National Defense Act of 1920, passed in the aftermath of the war, confirmed the results of 1916. Once again the War Department put forth a proposal that would have ended the Guard's front-line reserve role. This was the Baker-March bill, which would have established universal military training in order to provide a pool of trained manpower with which to expand the Army in wartime. It would have ended reliance on an organized reserve. The chairman of the Senate Military Affairs Committee, James W. Wadsworth, substituted for this a proposal to retain the Guard but convert it into a predominantly federal force. The Guard would have been under federal command in peacetime and available to the states for use in case of domestic emergency. The traditional relation between the federal government and the states with respect to command of the Guard would have been just reversed. The Wadsworth bill was killed in the House by a large bloc of antimilitarist congressmen from the rural Midwest, West, and South. Among the 212 members who voted against the bill, only 9 were from the Northeastern states. The NGA, which was badly disorganized as a result of the war, was less active than in 1916, and its lobbying does not appear to have been crucial to the outcome of the debate.[1]

For twenty years following the act of 1920, the Guard's

political life was remarkably tranquil. The Guard advanced no major new demands; the War Department mounted no new attacks upon it. Not until World War II was the Guard subjected to new political threats and spurred to fresh political activity, and then the result was to demonstrate how secure it had become. This period is not insignificant, however. The very stability of the Guard's political situation is in itself of some interest. This period is notable as well for the development of an important new political actor in the Guard's environment—the National Guard Bureau. Established in the War Department after World War I to administer Guard affairs, it has ever since functioned as an ally of the NGA.

SOURCES OF STABILITY

The reason why the Guard faced no challenges in these years is clear: until 1941, there was no war. On the contrary, there was in the United States a profound aversion to war, which was manifested in isolationist sentiment. The Army was subjected to popular indifference, even contempt, reminiscent of the late nineteenth century. Neo-Hamiltonianism, as Huntington has termed the militarist movement of the Progressive Era, died with the return to normalcy. Therefore the Army, though it was probably no happier with the Guard than before the war, was not in as good a position to challenge it. The Guard and the Army were once again, as in the period following the Civil War, united in defense against antipathy and indifference to military affairs.

The public record for this period is full of testimonials to the excellence of Army-Guard relations. Chief of Staff Douglas MacArthur grandly told the National Guard Association in 1932:

Your influence has contributed powerfully in combatting the rising tide of pacifism which threatens to engulf us. . . . I am anticipating another fight [on appropriations] the next session of Congress, and I cannot tell you the sense of confidence and security I feel in knowing that you will be standing shoulder to shoulder with me.[2]

The Guard did stand "shoulder to shoulder" with the Army

before Congress. In 1932, when a congressional committee suggested to the NGA that its demands could be financed by reduction of regular officer strength, the NGA demurred. This does not necessarily demonstrate altruism, since a cut in regular officer personnel would have reduced the number of inspector-instructors assigned to the Guard. It does demonstrate the defensive nature of the new rapport between the Army and the Guard.

The National Defense Act had taken some of the force out of the issue of federal control of the Guard. Though the Army undoubtedly wanted more authority over the Guard, it had gained enough in 1916 that new complaints would have to await new circumstances. In the meantime, Congress had made its preferences in military policy quite plain. The acts of 1916 and 1920 would stand until something—presumably a war—should challenge them.

One development of the Guard's environment did pose a threat in these years. That was growth of the Organized Reserves, a potential rival to the Guard. In 1916 a residue of the continental army proposal remained in the National Defense Act, thereby establishing, at the time inconspicuously, authorization for a reserve force wholly under federal control. This provision was reincorporated in the act of 1920, which stated that the Army of the United States was to be composed of "the Regular Army, the National Guard while in the service of the United States, and the Organized Reserves, including the Officers' Reserve Corps and the Enlisted Reserve Corps." Many officer veterans of World War I joined the ORC after the war. Subsequently its strength was sustained by graduates of the Reserve Officers' Training Corps, units of which were set up at colleges and universities under authorization of the acts of 1916 and 1920. There were 80,000 men in the ORC as of 1924. Like the Guard, the ORC formed a political adjunct, the Reserve Officers Association.

Once the ORC was established, the Guard had no choice but

to live with it. Doing so was not difficult as long as the ORC remained simply a pool of officers. The great virtue of the Organized Reserves, in the eyes of the Guard, was that they were not organized. Though statutory authorization existed for enlisted reservists, there were none. The federal reserve force could therefore not be formed, as was the Guard, into manned combat units. The NGA kept a wary eye open lest this situation change. In 1928, chiefly on the grounds that it would pave the way for creation of fully organized Reserve units, the NGA objected to a bill that would have established a War Department agency for administration of the Reserves. Though a version of the bill that was satisfactory to the Guard was finally submitted to Congress, objections from the floor killed it. Congress was no more eager than the Guard to see a vigorous federal reserve. This danger to the Guard, like challenges from the Army, lay dormant during the interwar period.

That the Guard should have faced no political challenges from rivals or opponents in this era of peace and isolationism is not surprising. That it should also have refrained from making important new demands is perhaps more in need of explanation.

One reason was the low level of its expectations for success. The Guard was discouraged from advancing new claims for federal support by the same environmental factors that discouraged the Army from issuing new challenges to the Guard. Almost as much as the Army, the Guard felt the inhibiting weight of public indifference to military affairs. Insofar as the NGA was active in these years, it was in an effort to get more appropriations. Although the National Defense Act authorized a peacetime strength of 425,000, during most of these years the Guard numbered between 150,000 and 190,000. Not until 1939, when the possibility of war could not be ignored, did Congress appropriate funds for a force of 210,000. At the same time, Congress passed a major piece of army legislation—the first in years —which gave the NGA an opportunity to acquire more federal perquisites. Realizing that the legislation was not likely to be vetoed, the Guard's lobbyist sought to add authorization of retirement pay for Guardsmen who suffered disability while in service. Despite objections from some congressmen, this amendment stayed in. This was the first legislation of significant material benefit to the Guard since 1916.[3]

Another explanation for the Guard's low level of political demands in this period is the *ad hoc* nature of the NGA's activity. The NGA still had no Washington headquarters or paid, permanent staff. It had a very skillful lobbyist in the adjutant general of Maryland, Major General Milton A. Reckord, but he spent only part of his time in Washington, and part of that was devoted to the National Rifle Association. In 1931 an Army general addressing the NGA observed that "this organization needs to be stirred up a bit as to its history." He had been unable to learn anything about it. In 1939 the NGA had only $7217 in the bank. A Princeton senior, at work on his thesis, concluded from Washington interviews that the Guard had ceased to be a force in military politics.[4] The NGA's lack of organization was of course partly a consequence of the Guard's low level of political demands. If the Guard had felt the need of a stronger lobby, it could have created one. The NGA could have imposed individual dues instead of relying on contributions of $3 per hundred members from each state Guard. The NGA's unexploited organizational potential was allowed to lie dormant. But the lack of a strong lobby was also a cause of the limited nature of the Guard's claims. If a permanent lobby had flourished in Washington, it would have had to proclaim new goals if only to justify its existence and satisfy Guard members that it was serving their interests. At least, this has happened in subsequent years, since a strong NGA has developed.

A third reason for the Guard's limitation of its demands is both more fundamental and more plausible than either of the two just advanced. This is the possibility that, as the Guard was growing older and more stable, a basic reorientation of its goals was taking place. Legislation already passed had secured its reserve role and provided it with large amounts of federal pay and equipment. Annual federal appropriations for the Guard were about $30 million a year, roughly twice as much as the states were spending. The Guard was now concerned to preserve what it had, and to develop political devices of self-protection.

Two matters did interest the Guard seriously in these years, and both were of such a kind as to support this interpretation. One of these was legislation to assure that Guard units would be kept intact in case of war; the other was development of the National Guard Bureau as protector of the Guard's interests within the War Department.

The provision of 1916 that in case of war Guardsmen should be drafted as individuals was offensive to the Guard. As soon as the war was over the NGA began asking for an amendment to eliminate this provision and make the Guard at all times, in peace and war, legally part of the Army. Advocates of this proposal argued that it would force the Army to take the Guard in units and give it greater security in its reserve role. On the other hand, such a change could imperil the Guard's status as a state force. General Reckord warned that if Guard officers were subject to Army discipline, the NGA would be muzzled. The Guard's problem was to find a way to lead a double existence— to be the militia, with the militia's constitutional freedom from federal control, and simultaneously to be part of the Army. After much study and debate, the NGA came up with a subtle solution to this problem. The Guard would have two legal lives, one as the National Guard of the States, the other as the National Guard of the United States. As the National Guard of the States, it would be organized under the militia clause and remain under command of the states in peacetime. As the National Guard of the United States, the same units would constitute a reserve component of the Army, organized under the army

clause of the Constitution and subject to an "order" to active
duty in case of emergency. These provisions were embodied in
National Defense Act amendments that Congress passed in
1933. They have been very helpful to the Guard in protecting
both its reserve role and its status as a state force.

In its effort to achieve security and construct protective
devices, the Guard was assisted as much by the passage of time
as by the passage of legislation. As it grew older, the Guard
sank roots deeper into the life of communities. When the Guard
burgeoned in the late nineteenth century it was a predominantly
urban institution. Now, with the aid of the automobile and of
federal funds authorized between 1900 and 1916, the Guard
spread into Main Street towns and rural areas. It developed ties
to the organizations that flourished there—the chambers of commerce, the Rotary and Lions clubs, the associations of mayors,
county treasurers, and other local officials. Such groups helped
the Guard to get reorganized after World War I, and when it
wanted something from Congress, they helped by sending telegrams. They were especially interested in getting funds for
Guard armories under the Public Works Administration program
during the Depression. Armories provided a place for community
activities—dances, garden shows, basketball games, and the
like.[5]

After 1920 the Guard had a strong ally in a newly formed
community institution—the American Legion. To a considerable
extent, the two organizations overlapped. Nearly all Guard
members joined the Legion. Legion positions on military policy
were favorable to the Guard and often hostile to the Army.[6]
The Guard had strong ties also to local business leaders. Again,
the two groups tended to overlap. Many high-ranking Guard
officers were among their community's leading businessmen. In
this period, as in the late nineteenth century, the Guard served
the interests of business in conflicts with labor. It saw frequent
service in strikes. In the pages of the *New Republic* and even

on the floor of Congress, it was attacked as the private army of big business. The CIO claimed that the Cleveland Chamber of Commerce made an annual contribution of $20,000 to the National Guard of Ohio. That the Cleveland Chamber and the Guard had close ties is clear. In 1936 the Chamber appointed as chairman of its military affairs committee Dudley J. Hard, a millionaire utility executive and newly retired commander of Ohio's 37th Division.[7] This case was probably not unusual.

Together, these various associations of the Guard helped to give it stature as a stable, continuing interest—one deserving of congressional concern and protection. A sizable number of Guard officers rose in these years to prominence in partisan politics. They were candidates for mayor, governor, and congressman. Not infrequently they won.

DEVELOPMENT OF THE NATIONAL GUARD BUREAU

Getting representation within the War Department had long been a problem for the Guard. This was one aspect of the general problem of maintaining control over its own fate. To safeguard a measure of autonomy became particularly important for the Guard as its dependence on the federal government increased. The National Defense Act of 1916 made federal administration of the Guard a large undertaking. It provided pay for forty-eight armory drills a year, prescribed federal standards for Guard officer personnel, and authorized the federal government to prescribe the units, by branch and arm, that the Guard should maintain. These functions, along with the issue of uniforms and equipment, constituted a broad area of federal responsibility for the Guard. It was crucially important to the Guard that these functions be administered by a sympathetic and highly accessible agency. It was also important to have an official spokesman before Congress. Until 1910, while relations between the Guard and the War Department were friendly and the two were pursuing the same goals, the secretary of war often performed this function. He endorsed the Guard's claims, thereby enhancing their legitimacy in congressional eyes. After the break with the War Department, the Guard had to rely exclusively on the NGA to present its views to Congress. In 1916 this had exposed it to embarrassing charges of playing politics. The NGA needed an ally with official status. The National Guard Bureau fulfilled these needs.

The evolution of the Bureau dates from 1903, when the Militia Act posed for the first time the problem of federal administration of the Guard. At that time militia affairs fell more or less by default to the assistant secretary of war. The incumbent happened to be a Guard officer and a student of militia policy. When he left, President Theodore Roosevelt appointed another Guard officer in his place. As a result, administration of the Guard was performed independently of the newly formed General Staff and by an official friendly to the Guard. When growth of militia business necessitated creation of a separate administrative bureau in 1908, it was made responsible to the secretary of war rather than the General Staff.[8] This situation changed in 1910. Within six days after Leonard Wood became chief of staff, he instructed the chief of the Division of Militia Affairs to report to the chief of staff instead of the secretary of war. Subsequently, under authority of an act of Congress passed in 1911, the Division was headed by a brigadier general who was an assistant chief of staff and a member of the General Staff. The effect of these changes was to tighten professional control over the Guard and to intensify conflict between the War Department and the Guard in the years before World War I. The militant members of the NGA demanded that a Guard officer be placed in charge of Guard administration.[9] In 1916 the National Defense Act removed the Militia Affairs Division from the General Staff and made it an independent bureau, responsible to the secretary of war. This was part of the larger effort by Congressman Hay and General Ainsworth to trim the powers of the General Staff. It was not the idea of the NGA, which wanted to add Guard officers to the General Staff.

How the Guard should be administered was one of the issues that Congress considered in 1920. The Guard itself was divided on the subject. One faction wanted to separate the Guard from the Army as sharply as possible. It would have created a bureau responsible to the secretary of war, entirely independent of the rest of Army administration, headed by a Guard officer, and advised by a council of Guard representatives from each of the states. Another faction of the Guard—which was concentrated almost exclusively in New York and headed by the commander of New York's 27th Division, Major General John F. O'Ryan— wanted to link the Guard more closely with the War Department. O'Ryan, a sponsor of the Wadsworth proposal to turn the Guard into a predominantly federal force, wanted Guard officers added to the General Staff ("brought into the club," in Wadsworth's phrase). O'Ryan thought that a Guard officer should head the Militia Bureau only if the Guard were converted to a federal status in peacetime. The War Department naturally favored the O'Ryan approach. That is, it favored adding Guardsmen to the General Staff, thereby reversing a position that it had taken in 1916.[10]

Congress solved this dilemma by giving the Guard the best of both proposals. It provided in the National Defense Act of 1920 that the Militia Bureau should be headed by a Guard officer, and it authorized Guard representation on the General Staff. Of these two provisions, the former was by far the more important. The nascent Militia Bureau, which was renamed "National Guard Bureau" in 1933, was just what the Guard needed to solve its problem of representation within the War Department. Ever since 1920, a major objective of the NGA has been to protect the independence of the Bureau, to enlarge its powers, and to assure its dedication to the interests of the Guard.

The rewards of this effort were apparent very early. The first

Guard officer to serve as chief of the Militia Bureau complained when he left office that the General Staff had interfered in his affairs. The NGA responded by having a bill introduced in Congress to define the Bureau's functions in law. This frightened the War Department into giving the Bureau chief a broad administrative charter. After 1926, he had "general administrative control of all War Department activities incident to the relationship established by law and custom between [the] National Guard and the Federal Government, except when the Secretary of War definitely assigns such activities elsewhere." Thereafter the Bureau dealt almost exclusively with an assistant secretary of war, independently of the General Staff and the adjutant general. It prepared and defended the Guard's budget. It administered Guard funds, which Congress appropriated to its account. It had custody of Guard personnel records and handled correspondence relating to the Guard. In the later words of one Army general, it became "an organizational monstrosity." [11]

Before World War I Guardsmen had argued that adequate representation of their interests within the War Department would make the NGA's activity unnecessary. Development of the Bureau did not, however, put the National Guard Association out of business. Instead, the NGA was strengthened by the addition of a partner, whom it viewed with jealous pride. They both appeared at appropriations hearings, one to present the official budget with restrained hints of dissatisfaction; the other, to amplify those hints into candid requests. [12] The Bureau became the Guard's source of information on events in the War Department—its eyes and ears—while the Association remained its spokesman. The Bureau supplemented rather than supplanted the Association.

This partnership was not without problems. Though Bureau chiefs and Association presidents did not become open rivals, conflict between them was a possibility of which Guard leaders were cautious. One reason that the NGA did not establish a headquarters in Washington in the interwar period was that the Bureau chiefs did not want it to.[13] There were also potential difficulties for the NGA in the selection of a Bureau chief. Rivalry for the office could become a source of dissension and personal jealousy. To mitigate this danger, the NGA has avowed a policy of not interfering in selection of the chief (this policy has not always been adhered to).

In conjunction with the War Department, the NGA tacitly established the principle that the Bureau chief should not serve more than one four-year term, even though the law allows him to. Law provides that the chief shall be appointed by the President, with the advice and consent of the Senate, from a list of officers recommended by the governors. In practice, the initiative for the nominations comes from the candidates themselves. An officer who wants to be chief tries to get his own and other governors to nominate him. In 1929, after serving one term as Bureau chief, Major General Creed C. Hammond solicited support for a second, with the result that all states but one nominated him. The dissenting state was Maryland, whose adjutant general, General Reckord, was the NGA's most powerful figure. Reckord told the War Department that a dangerous precedent would be set if, by obtaining nominations from all or most of the states, a chief could perpetuate himself in office. He argued that the governors were to "recommend officers, not elect them." The War Department agreed. In a letter to the President, the secretary of war pointed out that there were good reasons for limiting the chief to one term. The secretary did not elaborate on these reasons, except to say that the chief developed many contacts with the adjutants general in four years.[14] Restriction of the chief's personal influence was, it would seem, of common interest to the Army and the NGA.

Development of the Militia Bureau and the office of the chief was for the Guard the most important legacy of the National Defense Act of 1920. The Bureau contributed importantly to the Guard's autonomy. By comparison, the service of Guard officers on the General Staff was insignificant. Section 5 of the act of 1920 provided that "all policies affecting the organization, distribution, and training of the National Guard" should be made by General Staff committees to which "an equal number" of Guard officers would be added. An amendment in 1933 provided that there should be not less than five Guard officers on duty in the General Staff. Under these provisions, a Guard colonel or lieutenant colonel was ordinarily assigned to each General Staff section, and papers that affected the Guard were routed to these officers for comment. This procedure was not of much benefit to the Guard. Its representatives in the General Staff lacked the rank, legal authority, experience, or prestige necessary to exercise influence. After 1929 the standard tour of duty for Guard officers in the General Staff was only six months —too brief, the NGA argued, to permit effective performance. On two or three occasions, when a problem of more than routine importance arose, a joint committee was convened under Section 5—for example, in 1920 to plan army organization. The sporadic nature of these sessions limited their value to the Guard. Worse, there was a tendency for Guard representatives serving with regular officers in the General Staff to compromise their loyalty to the Guard. The Bureau, by contrast, was a permanently functioning staff unit. Its staff too suffered some conflict of loyalties—the chief especially was subject to competing pressures from the Army and the Guard—but the autonomous role of the Bureau conditioned even the regulars on duty there to become Guard partisans. (Most of the staff were regulars, since the law authorized only four slots, including that of the chief, for the Guard. As of 1929, there were twenty-six regular officers and eighty-four civilians in the Bureau in addition to the four Guardsmen.)

Although representation on the General Staff was less useful to the Guard than was the Bureau, it too had at least potential value as a protective device. Because this representation was authorized by statute, the Guard could complain to Congress, and thereby invite congressional action, if it were abridged. This happened during World War II. To surmount the war's political threat, the Guard used every means of protection already available, and in addition devised new ones.

THE POLITICAL DANGERS OF WORLD WAR II

In 1941, as at the turn of the century and in 1916, the country's involvement in military conflict opened the issues of concern to the Guard. This time the Guard did not stand to benefit from pressures for new military legislation. It had developed no new demands that the war might help to satisfy, but instead had developed an interest in keeping matters as they were. The war threatened to make this difficult to do.

The war's political dangers to the Guard—and the Guard's response—were foreshadowed in the Selective Training and Service Act of 1940, which threatened to supplant the Guard in the short run with a force of drafted men and in the long run with a trained federal reserve of dischargees. As the price of the Guard's support for the bill, General Reckord exacted from War Department officials and private sponsors, led by Grenville Clark, the "National Guard protective clause," which was incorporated in the opening paragraphs: "The Congress further declares, in accordance with our traditional military policy as expressed in the National Defense Act of 1916, as amended, that it is essential that the strength and organization of the National Guard, as an integral part of the first-line defenses of this Nation, be at all times maintained and assured." [15]

Even so, Reckord was not happy with the act. To the adjutants general he acknowledged, "it was only because of the necessity which confronted us at the time of great emergency that I felt we had to lay down and let the old steam roller run over us and grind a bill out." [16] To a small NGA convention the following month, after the Guard had been called to active service, Reckord pointed out that "the future of the National Guard is tied up in this thing," inasmuch as the draftees would be available following their discharge to constitute "a huge reserve army." He concluded that "you have got to keep your powder dry, you have got to keep men here on the job who see this thing as we see it and who will carry the fight, if necessary to Congress to see that the necessary legislation is provided to protect the National Guard as an institution." [17]

The National Guard took his advice. During the war the NGA sought to assure that the Guard's traditional existence— as a combat reserve force with a dual, federal-state status— would be protected. The principal target of its activity was the War Department, which was making postwar plans for military policy. This represented a significant change for the NGA. Always before the principal target of its influence had been Congress. The change was associated with the changing character of the Guard's goals. When those goals were predominantly offensive—that is, when the Guard sought new legislation—it naturally addressed itself to Congress. Now the Guard sought to prevent new actions, which were likely to originate in the War Department. It was important to stifle these actions at their source. To do so, the Guard exerted pressure both directly on the War Department and indirectly, through the threat of its influence with Congress. As a result it emerged from World War II with its traditional role and status explicitly reconfirmed.

The issue of who should make postwar policy plans for the Guard developed very early between the Guard and the War Department. The Guard wanted to plan its own future, or at least to have its future planned by good friends. The War Department thought that its own planners in the General Staff should deal with this problem. In the end, the Guard won. Its carefully nurtured autonomy proved invincible.

The United States had been at war for precisely a month when, on January 6, 1942, Major General George E. Leach—mayor of Minneapolis, former chief of the National Guard Bureau, and vice president of the NGA—urged Chief of Staff George C. Marshall to establish a joint committee of regular, Guard, and Reserve officers to study the postwar organization of the Army. The ordinary agencies of the General Staff, Leach wrote, could not give the problem the attention it deserved during the war. It should be considered instead by "a committee of able and experienced officers who are no longer required for active service."[18] Marshall replied noncommittally. He was obviously cool to Leach's proposal. Even the normal representation of the Guard in the War Department was suffering as a result of wartime reorganization. In March the National Guard Bureau was placed under the commanding general, Army Service Forces, depriving it of a valued position as a special staff agency with access to the secretary of war. Within another month, Guard representation on the General Staff under Section 5 of the National Defense Act was suspended for the duration. Yet the Guard and the War Department were not completely at odds over who should do postwar planning. Each wanted Brigadier General John McAuley Palmer to have a hand in it.

As a maverick Army colonel in 1920, Palmer had championed the citizen-soldier before Senator Wadsworth's committee. While the War Department argued for an end to organized reserve forces, he had sought a way to improve them and enhance their stature. Between the wars he wrote several books with the thesis that reliance on the trained citizen-soldier was the enlightened American tradition. As a consequence of his research and writing, he became the elder statesman of American military policy.[19]

The National Guard considered Palmer to be a man of rare vision. Late in 1941 NGA leaders asked him to come to Washington from New Hampshire, where he was living in retirement, and advise them on postwar plans for the Guard. At about the same time, General Marshall asked Palmer to serve as his advisor on postwar organization of the citizen forces. The two men had long been friends; Palmer was one of the few persons who addressed Marshall as "George." Knowing that Marshall in large measure shared his sympathy for the citizen-soldier, Palmer accepted, with the explicit understanding that he would be available as a consultant also to the National Guard.[20] One of Palmer's first actions was to endorse the Guard's request for formation of a joint Guard-Reserve-regular committee to study postwar military organization.

Palmer's influence was not altogether beneficial for the Guard. Although he believed deeply that the professional army should be kept at a minimum and that it should be supplemented by trained citizen-soldiers under the command of citizen officers, he also believed that the citizen-soldier should be unequivocally a creature of the federal government. He had favored establishment of a single federal reserve force after World War I but, in recognition of congressional attachment to the Guard system, he collaborated with Senator Wadsworth in drafting a bill that preserved the Guard's separate identity even while converting it into a predominantly federal force. With regret, Palmer witnessed defeat of that bill and perpetuation of the Guard's traditional status by the House of Representatives. In 1942–43, he began contemplating ways of setting right the error of 1920.

Palmer concluded that air warfare had made obsolete the rigid Guard system of training, on a territorial basis, large units that required lengthy mobilization time. Assuming that there would be a system of universal military training, he proposed that henceforth reservists be called individually. All would be under federal control. To the Guard would be left the task of home defense. Palmer observed that this had assumed new urgency with the arrival of air warfare. "Here," he wrote, "is a new military mission of the greatest importance—and one that might be suited to a force organized with a dual status . . . under the Militia Clauses of the Constitution." [21]

Palmer and other Army officers who were contemplating this scheme were faced with the difficulty of getting Congress to agree. The War Department, in its innocence, supposed for a short while that the solution lay in getting the Guard to concur in the plan. The Guard, it was thought, might agree to being abolished if it could help plan its own abolition. On the following recommendation from an Army colonel, a Guard officer was added early in 1944 to the Special Planning Division, which had charge of postwar policy planning:

6.   Delay in joining hands with the National Guard and their spokesmen in Congress in an attempt to encourage their whole-hearted support of the planning assumption mentioned in paragraph one ["elimination of the National Guard as now provided by law"] will only serve to widen the breach to the point where it cannot be bridged.[22]

Palmer considered bypassing Congress altogether. He observed to a friend late in 1943 that "the National Guard problem is one of many problems connected with our future military policy that simply cannot be solved if they are thrown willy-nilly into the Congressional hopper in the old way." He hoped that Congress would authorize a "commission of able civilians" to study military policy problems and submit a "coordinated solution" to Congress.[23] Whether Palmer pressed this idea on his congressional acquaintances is not clear. If he did, the chances are that he only intensified the interest of Congress in postwar policy planning. In 1944 the House established a Select Committee on Post-War Military Policy (the Woodrum Committee) to hold hearings on, among other problems, organization of the civilian components.

THE GUARD'S TACTICS

It was unrealistic of Palmer to suppose that Congress might be bypassed in military policy matters. With respect to the Guard, there was no way to achieve the War Department's objectives except by repealing or amending provisions of federal law. Only Congress could do this.

That Congress would be unwilling to do it was beyond doubt. There is ample evidence of congressional interest in the Guard in the wartime pages of the *Congressional Record*. Actions of Guard units are chronicled. There too, in remarks by Senator Bennett Champ Clark of Missouri, is a violent protest against the alleged "conspiracy" of the Army to destroy the Guard. (Clark had served as president of the NGA in 1919.)

Concern over the Guard was expressed in committee hearings. At the first session of the Woodrum Committee, Representative William J. Miller of Connecticut gently warned General Palmer against abolishing the Guard. In the War Department Appropriations Subcommittee the Guard also had good friends. "I can vouch for the fact that the interests of the Guard are in good hands," a committee member told a Guard witness in 1943. "We feel like we represent their interests, too, General." Two years later, a different member of the same committee observed, "We have always felt that the National Guard was our baby and we have done everything possible to build it up." [24]

Should the War Department propose action that would damage the Guard's interests, the Guard need only appeal to Congress for protection. In early 1944, the NGA informed the War Department that it was prepared to do just this. A group of Guard political leaders met with the War Department's policy planners in February. The Guard delegation was led by the aggressive new president of the NGA, Major General Ellard A. Walsh, the adjutant general of Minnesota; Governor Edward Martin of Pennsylvania, a former NGA president; and Major General John F. Williams, chief of the National Guard Bureau.

Palmer and Brigadier General William F. Tompkins, chief of the Special Planning Division, spoke for the War Department. Walsh made it clear that the NGA would insist on retention of the Guard in its dual status, organized as always in local units. In view of their attitude, Tompkins concluded in a memorandum to General Marshall, any attempt to change the Guard system would "inevitably (and probably fruitlessly)" provoke controversy in Congress.[25]

In addition the War Department was concerned to have the Guard's support for universal military training. This could not be taken for granted; the NGA had always been suspicious of UMT. If the War Department should antagonize the Guard, the Guard might retaliate by opposing UMT before Congress. The NGA had already threatened as much. At the Association's convention in 1943, General Palmer had spoken on behalf of a UMT bill that he was drafting in collaboration with former Senator Wadsworth, now a member of the House of Representatives, and the American Legion. Long an advocate of UMT, Palmer hoped to get the bill passed during the war while nationalist sentiment was at a peak. General Reckord demanded that it include the National Guard protective clause. "Your poor old Bill will be killed," Reckord told Palmer. "I happen to know through connections I have in the American Legion just how this whole thing has been set up, and I do not like it a damn bit." UMT lay at the heart of all of the War Department's postwar plans. Adoption of UMT was the assumption on which all other assumptions were based, the goal to which all other goals were subordinate—and the plain fact was that Congress would not pass UMT if the Guard were opposed. Retention of the Guard was therefore rationalized on the grounds that UMT would be secured and would, in turn, make the Guard worth retaining. This decision was approved by Secretary of War Henry L. Stimson.[26]

The NGA had achieved its principal goal with no more than

a private warning to the War Department that there would be a fight in Congress. It had successfully invoked the power of Congress without making a formal appeal for help. Nevertheless, the threat to the Guard had not passed. It remained for the War Department to draft specific plans for the postwar Guard—to define its mission and plan its strength and organization. In these matters the War Department might exercise considerable discretion within the limits of existing statutes. Even after Generals Palmer and Tompkins had agreed that the Guard must be continued in its dual status and had gotten Secretary Stimson to concur, they contemplated using it mainly for domestic defense, for example in manning coastal fortifications and anti-aircraft installations. The Guard had to find a way to influence the Department's planning if it were to retain its front-line combat role.

One source of protection for the Guard was the National Guard Bureau. In April 1944 General Tompkins asked the Bureau for recommendations on the Guard's postwar mission, and he gave guidance that strongly indicated a more limited mission than front-line combat. True to its role as a defender of the Guard's interests, the Bureau replied in late June that the Guard would not tolerate this idea. General Tompkins thereafter was reconciled to continuation of the Guard as a combat component. When Lieutenant General Lesley J. McNair and his successor as commanding general of the Army Ground Forces, Lieutenant General Ben Lear, both recommended in the summer of 1944 that the Guard be abolished or assigned domestic missions, Tompkins advised General Marshall to reject these recommendations.[27]

Helpful though it might be, the Bureau was not fully adequate to the Guard's needs. What the Guard really wanted was a controlling share in planning its own future, and the Bureau, being an administrative agency, did not have that kind of authority. In the spring of 1944, the Guard decided to renew its appeal for formation of a General Staff committee of Guard and regular officers to plan postwar policy for the Guard. That was what General Leach had asked General Marshall for in 1942. This time the Guard decided to carry its appeal to Congress.

In May 1944 the NGA president, General Walsh, submitted a long statement to the Woodrum Committee. He opened with a plea for preserving the Guard in its traditional form and with its traditional function, and then went on to complain that the War Department was violating an act of Congress (Section 5 of the National Defense Act) by not including Guard officers in postwar planning. The War Department responded obligingly. In August 1944 it set up a joint committee of Guard and regular officers to draft postwar policy for the Guard. General Palmer was partly responsible for this. He had helped Senator Wadsworth draft Section 5 in 1920, and he subsequently developed considerable pride of authorship in it. He advised General Tompkins that, notwithstanding the offensive tone that General Walsh had taken toward the Army, the NGA was right in claiming that a joint committee should be set up.[28]

The joint committee proved to be of great benefit to the Guard. Within a month after being appointed it began turning out policy statements that nicely suited the Guard's interests. It is not clear why this happened. The membership at first consisted of three regular and three Guard officers, each with the rank of colonel or lieutenant colonel; it would seem logical that they should have disagreed and become deadlocked. Instead, two regular officers joined with the Guard members to form a five-to-one majority in support of the Guard. Perhaps the Guard members proved to be dominant because they were better briefed and more aggressive. Or it may be that the whole committee was strongly influenced by a statement from General Marshall issued as a War Department circular on August 25, 1944, which Palmer wrote. With considerable eloquence,

Palmer distilled in this paper the basic arguments for building the country's military forces on an organized citizen reserve. The circular concluded that this policy would "be made the basis for all plans for a post-war peace establishment." The Guard stood to benefit from this circular even though Palmer's phrases did not apply explicitly to it (the circular avoided the question of whether the organized citizen reserve should be wholly under federal control). Another influence on the committee was probably General Walsh. Four days after the committee was established, he and other Guard officers appeared before it to present their views.[29]

In mid-September 1944, not long after publication of the War Department circular and the meeting with Walsh, the five-man, pro-Guard majority of the joint committee proposed to the chief of staff that the Guard be "an integral part and first-line reserve component of the postwar military establishment," and that it have the following mission:

To provide a reserve component of the Army of the United States, capable of immediate expansion to war strength, able to furnish units fit for service anywhere in the world, trained and equipped:

a. To defend critical areas of the United States against land, seaborne or airborne invasion,

b. To assist in covering the mobilization and concentration of the remainder of the reserve forces,

c. To enable integration, by units, into larger organizations or task forces.[30]

This statement secured the Guard's interests. After it was approved in October by the chief of staff and the secretary of war, other policies followed from it, and all were uniformly favorable to the Guard. The Guard's strength, the joint committee said,

should be determined by the "M" Day requirements for integration with, and supplementation of, the Regular Army, in order to form a balanced force ready for immediate deployment anywhere in the world.

Organizations allotted to the Guard, the committee agreed, should be those types which are required for the accomplishment of the mission of the NGUS and should conform in general to the troop plan of the War Department in order to insure an overall balanced force within the Army of the United States.

In one statement after another the committee confirmed the Guard's front-line combat role, and the National Guard Bureau echoed approval. While acknowledging that the mission proposed for the Guard was "extremely ambitious," the Bureau chief argued that it would be "possible under the assumptions announced"—that all Guard members would be graduates of a UMT program.[31]

With respect to administration, the joint committee recommended that the National Guard Bureau be restored to its prewar position as a semi-autonomous operating agency and that the Guard's representation in the General Staff be expanded and made more effective. Not only would the Guard have lieutenant colonels assigned to the General Staff sections (as it had before the war, under Section 5), but a new Section Five Committee would be created, composed of high-ranking officers who would meet semi-annually in the War Department to prepare policies relating to the Guard. One Guard member would be continuously on duty in the General Staff and would keep other Guard members informed. (The rank of Section Five Committee members was not specified, but all have been generals except the resident member, who is a full colonel.)[32]

These recommendations had all been worked out in at least rough form by the late spring of 1945. Meanwhile, a similar joint committee had been drafting policy for the Reserves. In midsummer, General Marshall decided to merge the committees and enlarge their membership with officers of high rank. To head the new committee he picked General Reckord, who for twenty years had been the Guard's lobbyist. This may have been done on the recommendation of General Palmer, who

knew both Reckord and Marshall well, or Marshall may have
picked Reckord on his own initiative. Presumably, Marshall
was seeking to add to the stature of the joint committee by
naming as chairman a general officer widely recognized as an
able spokesman for a reserve component. Reckord returned
from Paris, where he was serving as provost marshal of the
European Theater, in time to put the finishing touches on a
policy statement that secured the Guard's interests in the most
explicit way possible. He contributed a clause that committed
the federal government to providing armories for the Guard
(insofar as it could be committed by the War Department).[33]

With promulgation of this policy statement by the secretary
of war in October 1945, the war's threat to the Guard ended.
For a group so well established in law and tradition, and so
well armed with protective devices, self-preservation had
proved easy. Above all, the Guard had benefited from the support of Congress. It was the evident willingness of Congress to
protect the Guard that enabled the NGA to influence the War
Department.

THE "NEW" NATIONAL GUARD ASSOCIATION

There was one very important by-product of the Guard's
efforts at self-defense during World War II. This was the birth
of a vigorous and vocal lobby. The modern National Guard
Association dates from 1944—or, more accurately, from the day
at the 1943 convention when Ellard Walsh became president.
Walsh took office with the understanding that henceforth there
would be no hesitation to engage in political battles with the
Army. During a post-convention trip to Washington, he was
sure he saw a battle looming. Army officers had told him, so
he recalled years later, "This time we'll smash the goddamned
National Guard." He determined to launch a political counter-
attack.[34]

Walsh thought of a good many things to do in the Guard's

defense, some of which have already been described. To put life into the NGA was perhaps the most obvious. The NGA had never been a fully developed organization. Now, when the need arose, a zealous leader set out to make it one.

First he prepared a summons to political action. He spent nine months drafting his speech for the NGA's convention in May 1944. It was a history of epic battles between a single villain—the professional army—and a whole set of heroes—the Guard leaders who since 1879 had allegedly kept the citizen-soldier tradition alive with their activity in the NGA. For 145 closely printed pages covering 155 years (and condensed for delivery at the convention), Walsh recounted the Army's abuse of the Guard. Condemning professional officers variously as "Brahmins," "Bourbons," and "Samurai," he charged them with "undiluted and undisguised hate of us." West Point he castigated as "the root of all evil." He declared, mixing his metaphors, that the Army had "sowed the dragon teeth of conflict" and would "reap the grapes of wrath." In conclusion, he charged that the Army was engaged "in a diabolical attempt to destroy a great citizen force." To combat this conspiracy, he proposed that the NGA establish an office in Washington with a full-time staff.[35]

In the fall of 1944, with $11,000 of his own money, Walsh rented a Washington hotel suite for the NGA. By April 1945, he had collected $29,409 for its support from twenty-eight states. This appears to have come from the state treasuries. The NGA did not make a systematic attempt to get money from Guard officers on active duty.[36] From his own office in St. Paul and from the NGA hotel suite, Walsh issued a heavy flow of propaganda, including replies to adverse publicity about the Guard. Except for a couple of pamphlets, the NGA had never before published anything but a few convention proceedings. Now it published the 1944 proceedings in large numbers, a joint declaration of policy with the Adjutants General Association, and speeches by the governors of Iowa and Maryland, both of which the NGA had inspired.

General Walsh also maneuvered privately for political support. He got officials of the American Legion to agree early in 1944 not to support a UMT bill that did not include the Guard's protective clause. More surprisingly, he concluded a pact with the president of the Reserve Officers Association. On June 3, 1944, the two men signed a "joint statement of policy and pledge of mutual assistance" that: declared that "the citizen-soldier must be the major dependence of the Country in time of emergency"; endorsed the National Defense Act (especially Section 5); and affirmed, somewhat ingenuously, that "the interests and responsibilities of the Civilian components are identical." [37]

All of this activity may have had an impact on the War Department, in whose archives evidence of it is preserved. Yet it was, for the time being, mostly superfluous. When General Walsh summoned the Guard in May 1944 to combat the Army's "conspiracy," the War Department's decision to retain the Guard in its dual status was already two months old. General Walsh may have issued his warning partly in ignorance (there is no evidence that he knew of the War Department's decision). In any case it is not likely that he would have withdrawn or altered his massive summons to political action. He had in mind not just the issues of the moment, but the long-term defensive goals of the Guard. The NGA was to be one more protective device—the linchpin of them all—to withstand future challenges.

Challenges probably lay ahead, but the immediate postwar goals of the Guard were of a less dramatic sort. As usual after a war, the Guard had to get reorganized. It needed men, money, and equipment in larger quantities than ever before. Thanks to the political skill of the NGA, led by Generals Walsh and Reckord, it got them.

For several years after World War II Generals Walsh and Reckord, as leaders of the NGA, dominated federal decision-making with respect to the Guard. As a result the Guard stayed alive not only on the statute books, but also as a well-provisioned military force. In 1949 General Walsh could say with ample justification that "I am not being boastful, but . . . in providing wherewithal we have really become experts." [1] The following were the principal accomplishments of the NGA:

Manpower. Early in 1947 the NGA persuaded Congress to allow expenditure of $1 million for an intensive public relations and recruiting campaign. In the featured month of the campaign, 81,648 Guardsmen were recruited. Expenditures of the National Guard Bureau for public relations remained at about $1 million annually for three years. When the Selective Service Act was passed in June 1948, the NGA got Congress to provide that men who enlisted in the Guard between the ages of seventeen and eighteen-and-a-half and continued to serve satisfactorily would be exempt from the draft. For the next nine years, this source of manpower sustained the Guard.

Materiel. Immediately after the war, competition developed between the Guard and Reserves for materiel. The NGA got the War Department to issue a "clarification" of reserve policies that established the priority of the Guard. Shortly thereafter it prevented passage of a bill that would have authorized forty-eight armory drills a year for all Reserve units, the same number as authorized for the Guard.

Personnel Benefits. In cooperation with the Defense Department and the Reserve Officers Association, the NGA persuaded Congress to pass the Army and Air Force Vitalization and Equalization Retirement Act of 1948, which authorized retirement pay for non-disabled Guard officers. (The act also included benefits for regular and Reserve officers.)

Appropriations. In 1947 and 1948, which were stringent years for American military forces, the NGA got Congress to add a total of $79 million to budget requests for the Guard. In 1948 the Guard item was the only one in the Defense Department budget to be increased; Reserve funds were untouched, all others cut.

Autonomy. The first postwar years produced a series of threats to the autonomy of the Guard. Merger of the Guard and the Reserves was proposed by one or two officials of the Reserve Officers Association and by Major General Harry H. Vaughan, the President's military aide, who was a Reserve officer. In mid-1948 a Defense Department committee on reserve policy (the Gray Board), which Secretary James V. Forrestal set up in November 1947, recommended that the Guard and Reserves be combined in a single federal reserve component.[2] The threat of NGA opposition prevented the Defense Department from proposing this to Congress. And when the Air Force made independent efforts to gain greater control over the Air Guard, which was established as a separate reserve component in 1947, the NGA thwarted it time and again. In 1947 the NGA got Congress to provide in the National Security Act that the Air Force must administer the Air Guard through the National Guard Bureau ("the channel of communication between the Department of the Air Force and the several States on all matters pertaining to the Air National Guard," the statute said). When the Air Force tried to establish in each state an air adjutant general coequal with the army adjutant general, or, failing that, an Air Guard officer who would have the same rank as the adjutant general and who would take no orders from him, the NGA led the Guard in refusing to cooperate. When the Air Force, with the concurrence of the National Guard Bureau, in 1948 issued a directive claiming "tactical as differentiated from administrative command" over Air Guard units while in training for their federal mission, the NGA successfully opposed the directive and substituted another that gave the Air Force "training supervision as differentiated from command jurisdiction" over the Air Guard, thereby preserving the principle of state command in pristine clarity. When the Air Force seemed about to propose complete federal control of the Air Guard late in 1948, the NGA took a series of countermeasures that appear to have killed the proposal. Finally, in 1949, the NGA got Congress to endorse explicitly the dual status of the Air Guard in the Army and Air Force Authorization Act. This was a major political defeat for the Air Force, which until then had consistently enjoyed victory on Capitol Hill. Savoring his success, General Walsh made the following entry (March 18) in his diary:

General Reckord called from Baltimore and advised that the National Guard Legislative program seemed to be in excellent shape. He also advised that he had conferred yesterday, at length, with [Air Force] Secretary [W. Stuart] Symington, who intimated the U.S. Air Force would be disposed to drop their federalization efforts if the National Guard would agree to have the Air National Guard train in its NGUS status for a period of 45 days in each calendar year. . . . Advised General Reckord that in view of the action of the House, on H. R. 1437, there appeared to be no good reason why the Guard should make any concessions to the Air Force. . . .

The triumph over the Air Force in the federalization dispute marked the peak of the NGA's effectiveness, according to General Walsh, whose judgment on this point is surely authoritative.[3]

In the years immediately following the war the Guard was a highly motivated group with interests sharply defined and strongly felt. Its foremost goal was an obvious one: self-restoration. The men who were most strongly attached to this goal were the Guard's veteran leaders, general officers who were or had been division commanders and adjutants general. In effect they constituted the National Guard as a pressure group. They were members of a Guard generation that had joined after the Spanish-American War, served in World War I as company and field grade officers, and reached general officer rank in the thirties and forties. Generals Walsh and Reckord, who were their political spokesmen, epitomized this Guard generation.

Born in Canada in 1887, Walsh crossed the border into Minnesota as a small boy. He joined the National Guard in 1905 at the age of eighteen. Through acquaintance with a grocer's son who was a fellow Guardsman, he got a job in a wholesale grocery store and hoped to learn the business, but World War I took him into active service and speculation in sugar ruined the grocery store. When he returned home as a first lieutenant following thirteen months' service overseas, he had to find a job. Deciding to join an uncle who was mining in Alberta, he bought a railroad ticket and was about to leave the United States when he encountered his wartime colonel in downtown Minneapolis and learned that the governor would like to see him. Walsh did not know the governor, whom he had met only one time (while serving in an honor escort at a liberty bond rally), but the governor offered him a job in the administration of Minnesota's World War I bonus. The men who had been administering it, Walsh later recalled, were on the verge of creating a scandal that the governor could ill afford. Walsh took the job and became chairman of the Bonus Review Board, serving under the state auditor, treasurer, and adjutant general. In

1921 he received almost simultaneously an offer from the treasurer to become his deputy and one from the governor to become assistant adjutant general. "I decided," General Walsh related in 1960 with a touch of nostalgia and of drama, "to go military." He became acting adjutant general in 1925 and was promoted to adjutant general in 1927. In 1940 he took command of the 34th Division of Iowa, Minnesota, North Dakota, and South Dakota. (It was possible to be both an adjutant general and a division commander.) In February 1941 he went with his division to Camp Claiborne, Louisiana, but before long sought retirement from active service on account of a stomach ailment. He continued in office as adjutant general of Minnesota.

Reckord was born in rural Harford County, Maryland, in 1879, attended high school in the county seat, Bel Air, a town of some 1000 persons roughly twenty miles northeast of Baltimore, and joined the National Guard unit there in February 1901, when it was reorganized after the Spanish-American War. He entered federal service as a major in World War I, leaving behind a milling and grain business in Bel Air. He returned home a full colonel, the commander of Maryland's 115th Infantry Regiment. For leading the regiment in three weeks of combat north of Verdun, he had been awarded a Distinguished Service Medal and the French Croix de Guerre with Palm. Demobilized in 1919, he had resigned from the Guard and resumed his milling business when Governor Albert C. Ritchie offered him the office of adjutant general. When World War II began, Reckord was also commander of the 29th Division of Maryland, Pennsylvania, Virginia, and the District of Columbia. Overage for a combat command, he headed the Third Service Command in the United States until December 1943, when he became provost marshal of the European Theater of Operations. His active duty closed in 1945 with work on the War

Department's statement of postwar reserve policies. At the war's end, he had two oak-leaf clusters for his Distinguished Service Medal, a second French Croix de Guerre with Palm, a French Legion of Honor, and a British award as Knight Commander of the Order of the Bath. In November 1945, at the age of sixty-six, he resumed office as Maryland's adjutant general.

Generals Walsh and Reckord and others of their generation were men with lifelong stakes in the Guard organization, some of whom, as full-time members of state staffs, depended on it for a livelihood, and all of whom were bound to it by a sense of tradition and shared experience. They were also bound by a shared hostility to the professional army and a shared outlook on politics in general.

Seeking in 1947 to account for the Guard's hostility to the Regular Army, a General Staff colonel wrote: "Factors . . . include . . . a deep-rooted antagonism of many years standing on the part of certain older National Guard officers. The situation will be alleviated as these older officers disappear from the scene." [4] This antagonism was manifested primarily in the speeches of General Walsh. Its sources are not obscure. For one thing, this generation of Guard officers could recall the War Department's attempt to supersede the Guard with the continental army in 1916. They were too young then to be politically active, but they began to attend NGA conventions immediately after the war when memories of the continental army proposal were still fresh. General Walsh was secretary of the NGA in 1926 when the president was General J. Clifford R. Foster, leader of the Guard's fight against the continental army in 1916. In several long talks, Walsh heard Foster reminisce about the fight. Foster had been embittered by it and by the failure of the War Department to mobilize him in 1916, which he believed to be deliberate punishment for his political activity. [5]

General Walsh and his generation inherited hostility to the Army. Not they, but their predecessors, made the charge of "conspiracy" a vocal habit of the NGA.

It was not "conspiracy," however, that rankled most with the Guard. It was contempt. The greatest burden in the life of the Guard has been the contempt of the professional for the amateur. It is more a psychic than a political burden: the Army has never come close to abolishing the Guard. It is the more difficult to combat precisely because it is not political. Political challenges the Guard can repulse; defending its pride is more difficult.

This contempt, though real and pervasive, is hard to document, for it has been obscured by official statements. Evidence of it exists in the low quality of instructors assigned to the Guard and in the low value that Army officers attached to such assignments. Between the wars duty with the Guard was regarded as damaging to an officer's career. When General Marshall was assigned to the Illinois Guard as a senior instructor in the early thirties, he regarded it as a serious setback and unsuccessfully appealed to Chief of Staff MacArthur.[6] And if the Guard was humiliated in peacetime, it was even worse treated in wartime. Of eighteen Guard division commanders at the beginning of World War II, only two retained their commands. (Not all of the removals were disputed by the Guard.) Even so sympathetic a regular as General Palmer could write sarcastically of the Guard's "amateur major generals."[7] General McNair in 1944 had piled insult on insult:

1. One of the great lessons of the present war is that the National Guard, as organized before the war, contributed nothing to National Defense. . . . Dependence on this component as a great part of the Initial Protective Force of our nation was a distinct threat to our safety. . . .
2. The history of the National Guard, since its last induction into Federal service and until sweeping reforms were made, was one of unsatisfactory training, physical condition, discipline, morale, and

particularly of leadership. As a reserve component, the National Guard provided general officers who were not professional soldiers and who, almost without exception, were not competent to exercise the command appropriate to that rank. . . . It is common knowledge that, during the mobilization period preceding Pearl Harbor the most serious factor in the low state of morale among the enlisted men of the National Guard was lack of confidence in the ability of their officers. . . .

3. The training experience of this headquarters for nearly four years has its most important lesson in the inadequacy of the National Guard in practically every essential. . . .[8]

To the Army's West Point-trained elite, proud of their monopoly on the esoteric skills of military command, the Guard officer was an absurd impostor. Though clothed in the uniform of the military profession, he remained in their eyes at best untrained for command, at worst a hack politician. Much of the Guard's intense postwar hostility to the Army was therefore defensive—a response to insult, an impassioned denial of inferiority.

Yet it would be a mistake to take this hostility at face value. Much of General Walsh's rhetoric was designed to serve the organizational needs of the NGA. Though the depth of his emotional commitment to the Guard cannot be doubted, his violent speeches were not spontaneous and uncontrolled. General Walsh's most extreme language was calculated to serve political purposes, both indoctrination of the NGA and intimidation of the Army. His hostility increased or decreased according to the needs of the moment. If some NGA conventions were rougher on the Army than others, it was because he decided in advance that they should be.

Insofar as the Guard's hostility to the Army was real and not merely rhetorical, it was admixed with a good deal of latent admiration and awe. The attitude of General Walsh and other top officers toward the Army was highly ambivalent. They were Guard officers, after all, primarily because they were attracted by the role, the symbolism, the mystique, of the military man. Some had served as officers in the Army; others may have had the chance but declined it (like General Reckord, who, though urged to "go regular" by General Palmer, thought it would be "too confining"); many others did not have the chance at all. The attitude of each varied with his personal aims and experience, but it was inevitable that the regular officer should remain in the eyes of the Guardsman the archetypal military man, the epitome of much that he himself aspired to. It seems quite clear that one of the incentives to leadership in the Guard and the NGA was the opportunity to associate with the great and near-great general officers of the Army—to dine with chiefs of staff and knock on their doors, to hear their voices on the telephone, to be invited by them to meetings—in short, to at least move in their world even if not as a fully accepted member of it, and share in the aura that surrounds such men.

There are evidences of the Guard officer's ambivalence in the Guard's frequent assertions, on one hand, that it was not highly conscious of rank, and its positively fierce reaction, on the other, to usurpation of high rank by the regulars. But the precise quality of this ambivalence is perhaps best conveyed by the following preface to a speech that General Walsh gave in 1949 to the Command and General Staff College at Fort Leavenworth. This was the same man who had assailed the "Brahmins" and "Samurai," who regarded West Point as "the root of all evil," who had promised the Army "an eye for an eye and a tooth for a tooth"—but in the sanctuary of the professional, he was awed and respectful:

My feelings, at the moment, I am afraid would be rather difficult to analyze, as I find myself in the somewhat unprecedented position of addressing a part of the student body of this famous institution. To be perfectly frank, I am overwhelmed. In years gone by, when I was an officer of the line, it was my hope that someday I would be a student at this college of higher military learning, but somehow that wish failed to materialize and thus, I lost a golden opportunity to

round out my military education. It is a rare and unique experience
for a layman to be accorded the privilege of addressing this body,
and I am very grateful to General Eddy, your distinguished Com-
mandant, for the opportunity to do so. Ever since I accepted his
courteous invitation, I have wondered just what I could say that
would be of interest and command your attention.[9]

Along with an ambivalent hostility to the Army, General
Walsh's generation of Guard officers shared a belief in limited
government. They were, by and large, conservative Republicans and Southern Democrats, oriented to the state capitols
and the county courthouses.[10] Most were members of the
American Legion, militant patriots, advocates of economy in
government, and suspicious of the New Deal, liberals, and
growth of the federal bureaucracy. The Guard had an ally in
the *Chicago Tribune,* which was the only major daily newspaper except those in St. Paul and Minneapolis to which General Walsh had easy access. The *Tribune* published several
editorials reflecting his views and offered him a chance to rebut
unfavorable publicity about the Guard that had appeared in
the *New York Times.*[11]

Among the political beliefs of Guard officers, the most deeply
held and vigorously expressed was a belief in states' rights. In
the vocabulary of the NGA, the words "sovereign" and "state"
were irrevocably conjoined. They existed as one expression.
Much of the Guard's states'-rights rhetoric must be discounted
as rationalization, of course. Men became believers in states'
rights because they belonged to the Guard rather than joining
the Guard because they believed in states' rights. General
Reckord, who had supposed rather casually in 1919, in testimony before the Wadsworth Committee, that federalization of
the Guard might be a good thing, had no sooner been made
an adjutant general than he became a militant defender of
state sovereignty. In 1949, with an air of disdain for federal
authority, he told an NGA conference: "Now just think of this
directive being sent down to a sovereign State that the Gov-

ernor of the State shall place an Air Force Officer on the State Staff . . . who will take no directions and no orders from the Adjutant General. . . . Can you imagine anything sillier?" [12] Nevertheless, not all of the states'-rights rhetoric may be dismissed on the grounds that it represented an attitude acquired from Guard membership, deriving from the organization's interests. Given their backgrounds in rural and small-town America of the early twentieth century, many Guard officers of General Walsh's generation, particularly those from the South and Midwest, were strongly predisposed to a belief in small, decentralized government. This belief was strongly encouraged and made articulate—but not fundamentally caused— by their stake in the survival of the Guard.

Suspicion of the federal government never prevented leaders of the Guard from seeking federal money for their own organization. The apparent inconsistency of their beliefs and their behavior seems to have been easily overcome. For one thing, though they were eager for federal financial support, Guard leaders remained stubborn in their opposition to federal control of the Guard. They wanted the money without strings. Second, they invariably argued that the Guard represented a good bargain for the federal government because it was partly supported by the states (the amount of state expenditures for the Guard has often been exaggerated by NGA witnesses before Congress). And, since the only alternative to the Guard was allegedly a bigger Army or a bigger federal reserve, they could assure themselves with the soundest of logic that the effect of federal support for the Guard was, on balance, to restrict rather than encourage the growth of federal power. They came very close to the paradoxical belief that the more federal money spent on the Guard, the better served was the principle of states' rights.

Here then—in this generation of Guard officers—was a cohesive and intensely motivated group, positively eager for vigorous political action. Its principal goal was clear-cut and beyond internal dispute: restoration of the Guard, in its dual status, as a healthy, autonomous organization. For realization of this goal, the Guard had a propitious political setting.

THE GUARD'S ENVIRONMENT

The political actors to whom the Guard had to address claims were few in number, highly accessible, and in general predisposed to respond favorably to the Guard's demands. These political actors were Congress, the National Guard Bureau, the Section Five Committee, and the secretary of war and Army chief of staff. (The National Security Act of 1947, which created the Air Force as an independent service and combined it with the Army and Navy in a single National Military Establishment, complicated the Guard's environment. The Guard, having been split into Army and Air Force components, had then to deal with the secretary of defense, two service secretaries, two chiefs of staff, and two Section Five committees. The effects of this change were not, however, fully felt in the period under discussion here.)

Congress was the principal object of the Guard's claims. It had ultimate if not proximate control over the matters of major interest to the Guard: appropriations, military manpower policy, and preservation of the Guard's dual status. These matters were handled by the Military Affairs committees (after 1947, the Armed Services committees) and by subcommittees of the Appropriations committees.

Gaining access to Congress has never been difficult for the Guard, and it has never been easier than in these postwar years. The conservative Republicans and Southern Democrats who were the Guard's best friends (because they shared its commitment to a limited federal government) were in control of Congress following the election of 1946. Traditional attitudes toward military policy lingered in the Military Affairs committees and War Department Appropriations subcommittees, which were accustomed to thinking of the Guard as a mainstay of United States military organization. For a brief time after the war there was in Congress and presumably in the country at large a sense of continuity with the past—a "return to normal"—that lightened the political tasks of the Guard, an institution rooted in the "normal" past. In addition, a number of individual congressmen at this time were particular partisans of the Guard.

The folklore of the Guard's success with Congress stresses the Guard's ties to the party system. The folklore includes references to "the Guard vote" and to officer appointments in the Guard as "patronage." It explains the Guard's political success simply: "Of course the Guard has power—it's full of politicians." Such remarks imply that congressmen may expect to be rewarded at the polls if they favor the Guard and punished if they do not, and that congressmen support the Guard because to do so creates patronage that can be used to help them or their home-state party organizations. The folklore contains elements of myth and reality that are hard to disentangle.

It is true that many Guardsmen have been active in partisan politics, and that governors have used appointments in the Guard for partisan purposes. The National Defense Act of 1916 was designed to curtail this practice. It prescribed standards for Guard officer personnel, and provided that federal recognition (acknowledgment that a Guard officer meets federal standards) should be extended by decision of a three-man recognition board, which is customarily composed of two Guard officers and one regular officer. As of the early postwar years, this process had not put an end to partisan influence in the appointment of Guard officers. The Army's Director of Personnel and Administration wrote in 1948:

Experience since the war has demonstrated that governors will not accept the decision of a Federal Recognition Board. Men have been selected by governors for general officer positions in combat units who have had no command experience whatsoever. . . . Refusal to give federal recognition has resulted in continual political pressure on the Department.[13]

In the same year, General Walsh noted in his diary that Governor-elect Earl Long of Louisiana was about to remove Adjutant General Raymond H. Fleming because he had been "too friendly to the opposition." The entry (March 3) continued, "It appears that early in the campaign Mr. [Leander] Perez, prosecutor for Plaquimine Parish, had been promised he could name the adjutant general if he would support Long."

The involvement of Guard officers in state party politics has not necessarily meant that Guard members could concert their votes for the purpose of promoting the political interests of the Guard at the federal level. Individual Guard members have often engaged in electoral activity on behalf of personal friends or party nominees, but not with the idea of electing "Guard candidates." They have not been in politics to promote the welfare of the Guard, but more typically, have been in the Guard to promote careers in politics. It is difficult to view the "Guard vote"—except, perhaps, under special and rare circumstances—as other than a myth. Until World War II the Guard never included more than 200,000 officers and men, and its strength was divided among all of the states and between both political parties. It is doubtful that enlisted men should be counted in the potential Guard vote, inasmuch as political activity on behalf of the Guard has been confined to the officers, and the highest ranking ones at that. Even among this small group, devoted as they have been to the Guard, their membership in the organization can scarcely have been the dominant influence in their voting behavior, if only because candidate races that overtly involve the interests of the Guard have been rare. Congressmen have been so uniformly sympathetic to the Guard that in most cases it would be hard for a Guard partisan, determined to vote the organization's interests, to distinguish one candidate from another.*

None of this, however, gainsays the fact that Guardsmen have long been among the politically active elite of their communities, and that the Guard armory drill, like the church dinner or the Kiwanis Club meeting, is a "natural" setting for politics to be discussed and opinions formed on the local level. Hence, in the eyes of members of Congress, Guard officers might influence votes, whether or not they in fact do, and so a prudent congressman would not offend the interests of the Guard if he could avoid it.

The Guard's involvement in state government and politics has benefited the Guard above all by facilitating close relations with particular members of Congress whose own experience in state politics has linked them to the Guard. Congress always includes some ex-governors who, as former commanders-in-chief of state Guard organizations, carry to Congress a feeling of loyalty to the Guard. Many former governors sat in Congress in the postwar years, among them Edward J. Thye, senator from Minnesota, whom General Walsh had served as adjutant general. No fewer than seven ex-governors sat on the Armed Services Committee, constituting more than half of its twelve-man membership. They were Styles Bridges of New Hampshire, George A. Wilson of Iowa, Leverett Saltonstall of Massachusetts, Raymond E. Baldwin of Connecticut, Richard B. Russell of Georgia, Harry F. Byrd of Virginia, and Burnet R. Maybank of South Carolina. In addition, Congress included several men who had

---

* That the myth of the Guard vote has sometimes been believed by Guardsmen themselves makes it no less of a myth. In 1956, the NGA president reflected seriously in his diary on the possibility that if the Eisenhower Administration were not more friendly toward the Guard, the Republicans would lose the forthcoming election. The implausibility of this is so great as to leave an impression that the NGA, at least as represented by that particular president, had created an illusion in order to comfort itself and confound others. Or perhaps the illusion was created by others and merely shared by the NGA.

combined long careers in the Guard and in party politics. The outstanding example was Senator Edward Martin of Pennsylvania, who had made his way simultaneously up the ranks of the Guard and the Pennsylvania Republican organization. Martin joined the Guard in 1898 at the age of nineteen. Several years later, after graduating from college, he entered politics as a county solicitor and secretary of the Republican county committee. By 1910 he was a member of the Republican state committee and a major in the Guard. After World War I, during which he reached the rank of colonel, he held state office as auditor general (1925–29), treasurer (1929–33), and adjutant general (1939–43), serving as Republican state chairman from 1928 to 1934. He was also president of the Gasoline Tax Collectors Association of North America and president of the Auditors, Controllers, and State Treasurers Association. By 1939 he was a major general in the Guard and commander of the 28th Division. In the early 1940's he was president of the National Guard Association. In 1943 he was elected governor of Pennsylvania. In 1947 he went to the Senate. Through Martin, the Guard had access to the majority leadership of the Republican Eightieth Congress. From these and other friends in Congress, the NGA could be sure of generous treatment on any issue. On occasion the Guard's friends, acting independently of the NGA, took the initiative in proposing defense of its interests. In 1948, for instance, Congressman Errett P. Scrivner of Kansas, a former Guardsman, questioned the NGA's wisdom in advocating a common federal commission for officers of the Guard and the Officers' Reserve Corps because he feared it would facilitate extension of federal control over the Guard.

The National Guard Bureau, like Congress but for different reasons, was an easy target for NGA influence. From the Bureau the NGA sought efficient and zealous pursuit of the Guard's interests. It urged the Bureau to be bold both within the War Department and before Congress in asking money and other resources for the Guard, and it exhorted the Bureau to speed in administering the postwar reorganization of the Guard. By tradition, and by virtue of the fact that its chief was a Guard officer, the Bureau was committed to serving the Guard's interests. Thus it was a natural ally of the NGA. But it was clearly a dependent ally. For success in administering the Guard and for its very existence, the Bureau was obligated to the NGA. When it wanted something from Congress—more money or more flexibility in the use of money—the Bureau turned to the NGA. Even within the Army, much of the Bureau's authority depended on its partnership with the NGA. When the Bureau spoke for the Guard's interests, its words were backed by the Association's weight. With the Bureau's dependence on the NGA went deference to the NGA's wishes.

Newly established after World War II, or at least established in new form, the Section Five Committee, composed of Guard and regular officers, sat infrequently and acted perfunctorily on the issues that came before it. But, because it had statutory authority over policies relating to the Guard, the NGA could insist that certain problems be channeled to it. The NGA then could easily influence the committee's deliberations. General Walsh occasionally had a voice in the nomination of Guard officers to the committee. The Guard members of the Committee were, like the Bureau chief, chosen by the secretary of war from among nominees by the governors. It was possible for the NGA to influence the nominations, if only by encouraging a particular officer to become a candidate. Walsh early developed the practice of briefing the Guard panel before committee sessions. Both he and General Reckord sometimes attended the meetings. In 1946 the Section Five Committee was the vehicle for a "clarification" of War Department reserve policies that asserted the Guard's priority over the Reserves.

The Offices of Chief of Staff and Secretary of War were courts of last resort for the NGA when things were going badly for the

Guard elsewhere in the War Department. As General Reckord explained to a congressional committee in 1947: "If anything goes wrong, General Walsh and I can walk in to the Chief of Staff or to the Secretary of War, because we are not in the chain of command. We go in and say to General Eisenhower, 'Here is what happened down in the Bureau.'"[14] Competition from the Reserves in 1946 was relieved partly by direct complaints to the secretary of war and chief of staff. In general, the NGA had easy access during these years to the very top of Army administration, and it seems always to have had a sympathetic reception there. In the testimony just quoted, General Reckord went on to say that the Guard had never appealed to General Eisenhower ("one of the grandest fellows in the world with whom to deal") or Secretary of War Robert P. Patterson without receiving a satisfactory response. The NGA's complaints about its treatment by the Army have usually been directed against subordinate officers. General Reckord told the NGA conference in 1946:

I have an exceedingly high regard for Mr. Patterson, General Eisenhower, General Handy, General Devers and General Spaatz [respectively secretary of war, chief of staff, deputy chief of staff, commanding general, Army Ground Forces, and commanding general, Army Air Forces]—they are leaders of whom we may well be proud. I enjoy their confidence and their respect. . . . However, these officers can do little more than determine the policies. . . . The details, of necessity, must be left in the hands of subordinates, and it is these subordinates who, notwithstanding their "honeyed words" and their "lip service," have prepared plans and issued directives which will—if carried out—destroy us.[15]

Blaming the "Indians" and not the "chiefs" may have been a deliberate NGA tactic designed to woo the chiefs (and intimidate them without seeming disrespectful); just as likely, it was an honest appraisal of the situation. Why top officials should have been so much more sympathetic to the Guard than their subordinates is not clear, but one probable explanation is that they were more sensitive to its political influence. In case of a public fight with the Guard, they would have had to do the fighting.

If the Guard was fortunate in having so few and such friendly objects of influence, it was fortunate as well in having few obstacles to success in the form of strong political opponents. The Reserves, a political rival, were in a pathetic condition. They could not get organized. This was partly because of faulty administration. Control over the Reserve program was scattered among sections of the General Staff and the Office of the Executive for Reserve and ROTC Affairs. Even after Congress passed a Reserve pay bill in July 1948, after NGA objections had been withdrawn, five months elapsed before money reached the Reservists. A House Appropriations Committee report in 1948 contrasted the Guard's success and the Reserves' failure.[16] In its controversies with the professional services—and specifically, in the battle with the Air Force over federalization—the Guard was engaged with more imposing opposition. But the Air Force was young and preoccupied with more important political matters. In December 1948, when the threat of federalization was at a peak, General Walsh noted in his diary the opinion of a fellow Guard officer that the Air Force would not want to fight the Navy and the NGA simultaneously. The bitter Air Force-Navy conflict over strategic programs that broke out in 1949 was already taking shape.

The Guard enjoyed, then, a generally favorable political setting. Potentially, this complemented the Guard's own sense of shared, sharply defined interests. The role of the Guard's lobby, the NGA, was to exploit these political assets, both internal and external. Along with a favorable setting and a favorable internal situation, the activity of the NGA was the third essential component in the Guard's extraordinary success as a pressure group.

The NGA, in the persons of Generals Walsh and Reckord, gave the Guard political leadership. They gathered information of concern to the Guard, defined its interests, communicated its position to Congress and the executive branch, and devised tactics for eliciting favorable action. To describe the activity of these leaders is to describe the NGA, for they *were* the NGA in this period. The organization was still in the early stages of development. To describe their political activity is also to illustrate the nature of the Guard and the extraordinary loyalty it evokes. Not every organization could have produced an Ellard Walsh and a Milton Reckord, who—notwithstanding the satisfaction that they probably found in political activity for its own sake—were motivated in large part by love of the Guard. They received no pay from the NGA in these years.

General Walsh, as president, was the organizer of the NGA, the exhorter to action, the propagandist for the Guard. To these tasks he brought many of the classic attributes of the Irish politician; had he been born in Boston, he might have been its mayor. His home was St. Paul, "Boston of the West." Gregarious, voluble, in love with political combat, he was above all endowed with the Irishman's fighting temperament.

Walsh had as well the Irish politician's flair for organization. Even as a young officer in the 1920's, he had been much interested in the NGA, and, partly on the strength of an exceptional memory for names, had been made its secretary. In 1928–29 he served a term as president. Now he invested the job with almost apocalyptic fervor. He laid plans for making the NGA an effective organization, and worked with enormous energy and determination to carry them out. In 1946 the NGA abolished the system of levying $3 in dues per 100 Guardsmen in each state and established individual memberships instead. (Dues were set at $5 for company grade officers, $7.50 for field grade officers, and $10 for general officers.) *The National Guardsman,* official monthly magazine of the NGA, was founded in March 1947 to inform and indoctrinate Guard officers. In addition, General Walsh continued to make lengthy, propagandistic annual reports to NGA conventions, which were enlarged after the war and renamed "conferences." For his role as propagandist, General Walsh was equipped with a garrulous nature and a religious sense of mission. His speeches were heavily laden with Biblical metaphor. "Our cause must indeed have been a righteous one," he told the NGA conference in 1946, "and an all-wise Providence guided our efforts, for otherwise those monstrous efforts to destroy us would have succeeded." [17]

General Walsh was seeking to influence mostly the younger officers, many of whom were new to the organization and very few of whom, in any case, had ever been active in the NGA. Usually he sought to unite them by stirring hostility toward the professional services, but he also made positive appeals to the Guard's pride. Guardsmen were told of the long history of their units, of the constitutional foundations of the Guard, of the wisdom of the founding fathers in planning for a militia, of the crucial role of the citizen-soldier in American democracy, and of the Guard's importance in the functioning of the American federal system.

It is difficult to assess the results of General Walsh's attempts at indoctrinating the Guard. Though his authority as spokesman for the NGA was never challenged, there is scattered evidence that some Guard officers, either deliberately or through ignorance, did not always follow where he led. Disagreeing with Walsh's attacks on the Army, one Illinois division commander refused to serve on an NGA committee in 1946. Several officers at the 1946 conference of the NGA objected to one particularly vengeful resolution that was aimed at the Army. An Army officer who reported on this convention to the General Staff believed that "the vindictive criticism expressed by the older National

Guard Association leaders who were in complete control of the conference was not concurred in by a number of younger troop leaders." [18] In 1948 some Guard members of the Air Section Five Committee sided with the Air Force in support of the Gray Board report, either because they were imbued with loyalty to the Air Force or because they were indifferent to the niceties of the militia cause. Enrollment in the Association during 1948, the first year of individual dues collection, was disappointingly small. Whereas the NGA committee on finance had counted on enrolling 90 percent of the eligible officers, only 48 percent had joined by September, leaving the Association with a deficit for the year.

Whether General Walsh succeeded in engaging the loyalty of his followers during the first years of the "new" NGA may not be very important. The fact is that by sheer personal aggressiveness he established himself as a fully authoritative spokesman for the Guard's political interests, and whether a majority of Guard officers acquiesced in his leadership out of apathy or followed him out of conviction was not at the time of great practical significance. Not much was immediately required of them except payment of dues, though in the long run they would be expected to produce skilled political leaders worthy to inherit the organization that Walsh was building. In the meantime, the older leaders of the Guard, Generals Walsh and Reckord and other officers of their generation, remained to provide political leadership—to hold committee chairmanships and other offices in the NGA and to occupy the offices of the adjutants general in the state capitols. This generation did not need to be indoctrinated.

General Reckord, as chairman of the NGA's committee on legislation, represented the Guard's interests to others. With help from General Walsh, he bore the burden of lobbying—the phone calls to congressmen and chiefs of staff, the drafting of bills and amendments, the composition of telegrams. He brought to this job long experience as a lobbyist, dating from the years after World War I.

Reckord had become involved in Guard politics accidentally, through a chance combination of personal acquaintance and proximity to Washington. In France during World War I he became friends with his brigade commander, Brigadier General John McAuley Palmer, and when Palmer returned to Washington in his role as champion of the citizen-soldier, Reckord was one of the Guard officers from whom he sought support and advice. Reckord was called to testify on Guard policy before Senator Wadsworth's committee in 1919. (He endorsed the Palmer-O'Ryan proposal for turning the Guard into a national force.) Within a year he was called to active duty with the General Staff as a member of the first Section Five Committee, a group of regular, Reserve, and Guard officers who planned the postwar organization of the Army.[19]

Having been introduced to Washington, Reckord soon began to feel very much at home there. Fellow Guard officers farther from the capital began routinely to ask for his assistance. "I could arrange things by driving over in one day and seeing the right man," Reckord recalled years later. "I could arrange things that irritated people all over the country. I would receive a note from some friend in the Midwest—maybe Charlie Grahl out in Iowa—saying, 'When you're next in Washington, I'd appreciate it if you would stop at the Bureau and straighten a problem out for me.'" By the middle 1920's, Reckord's operations in Washington had become more or less formal. In 1927 he succeeded Major General Fred C. Ainsworth, the redoubtable former adjutant general of the Army, as executive vice president of the National Rifle Association. After that, Reckord regularly spent half of his working days in Washington, driving back and forth from Baltimore and staying two nights each week at the Army-Navy Club in the capital. His time in Washington was divided among his office at the NRA, the War Department, and Capitol Hill.

His contacts increased with the years. Palmer and Pershing, Marshall and MacArthur, the young Dwight Eisenhower—all were his friends or acquaintances. He met MacArthur during World War I and came to know him better while the Third Corps Area, in which Baltimore was located, was under Mac-Arthur's command. He met Eisenhower in the 1920's when the future president was a major stationed at Camp Meade, Maryland. He met all of the interwar chiefs of staff routinely, in the course of conducting Guard and NRA affairs. To congressmen on the appropriations committees he was a familiar and welcome witness. All of the Maryland congressional delegation knew him well, and a few had served under his command. He had a friend, too, in John Thomas Taylor, the legislative agent of the American Legion, with whom he sometimes shared labors.

Reckord's skill and experience as a lobbyist grew along with the range of his acquaintance. He wrote most of the legislation relating to the Guard in the interwar years, including the National Defense Act amendments in 1933 (though these were formally the product of a special NGA committee). "I always went to Congress with a written bill or amendment," he recalled in 1960.

My secretary and I would bang it out and take it over to the chairman. Usually there were one or two Guard officers on the committee, and we would go to them or the chairman. When we had the bill about the way we would like it, we would have the chairman or some other friend introduce it, and then we would hold a hearing. . . .[20]

A different technique was required for preventing legislation harmful to the Guard. Here is Reckord's contemporary account of his handling of the Selective Training and Service Act in 1940:

In the Draft Act I personally did everything I could to secure the future of the National Guard. It just happened that, through a circumstance, two of the New York gentlemen who were on the Training Camps Association Committee, which was responsible for that Act, happened to be good personal friends of mine. . . . It happened that I was in Washington the day the bill was presented and was immediately advised and, on my way back to Baltimore that evening, I stopped by the Senate Committee room and picked up two copies of the Act and took them back to Baltimore. [He then explains that he and three members of his staff were busy studying the bill when he got a call from one of his friends in New York asking him to appear at the House hearing on the bill.] I said, "Well, I expect to be there, but I am opposed to your bill." He said, "My God, don't say that. We want you fellows to be with us." Then I heard him talk to some other gentleman who afterwards proved to be Mr. [Grenville] Clark, and finally he introduced Mr. Clark to me over the telephone, and Mr. Clark asked me to withhold my fire until they could see me the next day, which I agreed to do. . . . Well, the net result of that meeting was that I had to tell them, very frankly, that unless they amended the bill . . . I felt sure the Guard would have to oppose the legislation. . . .[21]

Reckord was less voluble than Walsh but more prestigious and more pragmatic, qualities that suited him for his more subtle and specialized role. His wide acquaintance with persons influential in the Guard's sphere of interest, his familiarity with statutes relating to the Guard, and his authoritative manner made him a lobbyist of incomparable effectiveness. "The most powerful man I have seen in fourteen years," a veteran member of the House Armed Services Committee staff said of him in 1960. "He had *tons* of connections and *no* hesitation to use them."

These two extraordinary men constituted the political leadership of the Guard. Occasionally they consulted with Senator Martin, whom General Walsh had succeeded as NGA president, or with other Guard officers of their own generation, but their dual domination of the Guard's political affairs was total. All of the labor of leading the Guard was divided between them. Their tactics varied according to their targets of influence, but some generalizations can be made about their lobbying behavior.

Above all, Generals Walsh and Reckord were alert and aggressive. They gave the Guard's interests constant attention;

not even minor matters were allowed to go by default. Knowing that this was so, congressmen and officials of the executive branch often checked with them routinely before taking action on Guard matters. Congressmen, especially, developed the habit of anticipating the NGA's claims. In a hearing of the House Armed Services Committee in 1950, a committee staff member asked Army Chief of Staff J. Lawton Collins whether the Guard had been consulted about an army organization bill. When Collins replied that drafts had been shown to the National Guard Bureau and the Section Five Committee, Committee Chairman Carl Vinson interjected: "What was the reaction of General Reckord? . . . Of course, you do not have to consult with them, but they will consult with us." [22]

Walsh and Reckord were tenacious and uncompromising. It was an axiom of political existence for Ellard Walsh that ". . . there can be no thought of appeasement or conciliation. Neither is there room for compromise." [23] His stubbornness, combined with that of General Reckord, made the NGA a very hard bargainer. This is perhaps best, because most boldly, illustrated by the NGA's attitude toward the selective service acts in 1940 and 1948 and UMT in 1943. A less forceful man than General Reckord might have hesitated to bargain for the Guard with a threat to kill the draft in 1940 or UMT in 1943. Less tenacious men than he and General Walsh would not have held out for such favorable measures as were given the Guard in the Selective Service Act of 1948. The bill originally proposed by the Defense Department would have exempted from the draft only those Guardsmen who were members as of the date of the act, and it would have broadened the Guard's protective clause to include other reserve components. In meetings with Defense Department officials, the NGA obtained a restatement of the protective clause in its original form, as well as a draft exemption for all men who joined the Guard between the ages of seventeen and eighteen and a half.[24] It cannot be said that either man was incapable of compromise. With respect to the draft act what they really wanted was a blanket exemption for all Guard members. They gave this up when General Reckord concluded that a partial exemption was all they could get. Like every other group that bargains for favor in Washington, the Guard under Generals Walsh and Reckord consistently settled for less than it asked, but even then it refused to admit as much. When they were conveyed by General Walsh to NGA conventions, all of the Guard's victories were total. He could compromise in practice, but he would not admit the principle.

Finally, Generals Walsh and Reckord were combative. Whether or not the Guard could be beaten on any given issue, it could not be beaten without a fight. Late in 1948, when the NGA suspected that President Truman might recommend federalization of the Air Guard in his forthcoming State of the Union message, General Walsh noted in his diary—probably with eager anticipation—that the National Guard and the states would "soon face the greatest fight of all time to maintain the integrity of the National Guard and the American way of life." The manifest willingness of the NGA to fight sometimes saved it from the necessity of doing so, for its potential opponents, the professional services, did not share its relish for political conflict conducted in public view. Besides, a fight with the National Guard never promised victory to anyone. In this case, the Air Force capitulated to the NGA following delivery of the State of the Union message without a recommendation for federalization. If the Air Force could not have the President as an ally, it would not fight. In the presence of General Reckord, Secretary Symington picked up his telephone and directed that action on legislation to federalize the Air Guard be suspended.[25]

It is difficult to separate the personal effectiveness of Generals Walsh and Reckord from their effectiveness as representatives of the National Guard. If they were aggressive in their assertion of the Guard's interests, reluctant to compromise those interests, and eager to fight in defense of them, the reason lies but partly in the aggressive, uncompromising, and combative natures of the two men. They were emboldened as well by the formidable political assets of the group for which they spoke. Chief among these was the continuing attachment of Congress to the Guard. That was the basis of their success.

The activity of Generals Walsh and Reckord was facilitated by an unusual degree of access to authority. The Guard, after all, is *of* the government. Spokesmen for its interests—the National Guard Bureau and the Section Five committees—possess formal authority within the Defense Department. The chief of the Bureau and the resident member of the Section Five Committee, a Guard colonel on active duty in the Pentagon, constantly fed political intelligence, a full supply of both fact and rumor, to Generals Walsh and Reckord. At the height of the conflict with the Air Force, the head of the Air Division in the Bureau relayed a rumor that the Air Force was about to rescind the October 1945 statement of reserve policies that it had inherited from the War Department. Alarmed by this threat to the Guard, General Reckord sent telegrams to Secretary Symington and Chief of Staff Hoyt S. Vandenberg urging that, pending a conference with the NGA, no changes be made in existing policies. The Air Force assured him that none would be.[26] Generals Walsh and Reckord also had prompt access to information in their official capacity as adjutants general. The state "AG's," as they are called, have a foundation in federal law. Partly by statute as well as custom, federal actions with respect to the Guard are communicated to the states via the adjutants general. Through these channels, Generals Walsh and Reckord learned promptly and automatically of administrative actions by the Army or Air Force. This helped them to take quick counteraction. When the Air Force tried in 1948 to assert tactical command over Air Guard units in training, General Walsh received a copy of this directive in his capacity as the adjutant general of Minnesota—and promptly objected that it was "unconstitutional, illegal, and a wholly wrong approach to the problem." General Reckord drafted a substitute.[27]

Without the prompt access to official information that the Guard's public character afforded them, Generals Walsh and Reckord would not have been able to act so effectively. On the other hand, not being subject to official discipline, they were free from authority's restraints. The NGA was able to range widely in exerting its influence because, in a favorite phrase of General Walsh, it was "free and untrammeled." Walsh and Reckord could go straight to the top of Army and Air Force administration or to Congress without asking the approval of anyone or fearing reprisal.

Their approaches and techniques varied with the object of their influence. Toward Congress they were friendly and even, at times, deferential. They did not threaten; they appealed. Acting (correctly) on the premise that Congress would protect the Guard's interests, they sought to show what action was needed for that purpose.

On any important matter they solicited assistance from adjutants general or from former Guard officers in Congress who could approach on a basis of friendship those individual members from whom action was sought. In the winter of 1946–47 the NGA was trying, at the request of the National Guard Bureau, to get informal approval from the House Appropriations Committee for spending $1 million of the Bureau's funds for a recruiting and public relations program. Consent was needed from two men: Albert Engel of Michigan, chairman of the War Department subcommittee, and John Taber of New York, chairman of the parent committee. The NGA summoned Adjutant General LeRoy Pearson of Michigan to Washington to talk to Engel. It approached Taber through Congressman Bernard M. (Pat) Kearney, a former Guard general who represented an upstate New York district not far from Taber's. Some years later

General Walsh recalled that Congressman Kearney "almost single-handed influenced Congressman Taber to approve the million-dollar publicity item." [28] The same technique was used when Congress was considering appropriations. As time for committee action approached, the adjutants general in states that were represented on the committee were asked to send telegrams. When the Selective Service Act of 1948 was under consideration, the NGA called all of the adjutants general to Washington to lobby. By the time they arrived the contents of the bill had already been agreed on, but it may be that knowledge of their impending arrival helped induce the Defense Department to make concessions to the Guard.

In general, the NGA worked through the Guard's friends in Congress and refrained from pressing congressmen to take a position toward which they were not already inclined. The NGA's action on universal military training illustrates this point. Formally, the Guard was allied with the War Department, American Legion, and the Reserves in supporting UMT in the immediate postwar years. The Guard needed UMT as a source of trained manpower. Nevertheless, the American Legion charged, with some justification, that the Guard's heart was not in the fight. The issue was embarrassing to the NGA because its best friends in Congress, the men with whom it maintained contact, did not believe in UMT. Mostly these were Midwestern Republicans who, like the Guard, favored limited government. Senator George Wilson of Iowa, one of the Guard's closest supporters, was an avowed opponent of UMT and criticized the NGA for backing it. Senator Robert A. Taft of Ohio, also a good friend of the Guard, opposed UMT. Senator Martin agreed to support it but was reluctant about the cost. Senator Thye told Walsh that he would vote for UMT but that he did not believe in it. When the Army approached General Walsh in February 1948 in the hope that he would reply to an anti-UMT speech of Senator Taft, he declined on the grounds that the Guard had made its position plain and that Taft's mind could not be changed anyway. The NGA was not willing to press its friends to vote for something they did not believe in.[29]

Toward the National Guard Bureau, by contrast, the NGA was not deferential, but imperious. The Bureau chiefs in this period (Major General Butler B. Miltonberger, 1946–47, and Major General Kenneth F. Cramer, 1947–50) had both served as line officers rather than as adjutants general, which meant that they were not as imbued with the state tradition of the Guard and with hostility to the Army as the NGA thought they should be. In particular, Miltonberger arrived in the Pentagon with an excellent combat record but considerable naïveté with respect to the Guard's political interests. The chiefs were often treated like errant children, in need of instruction and protection. On one day in 1946 General Walsh spent two hours indoctrinating Miltonberger and impressing on him the need for cooperating with the NGA.

In routine administrative matters the Bureau regularly took cues from the NGA. When Congress was considering appropriations for the Guard, officials from the Bureau and the NGA together decided what position to take in testimony. In the spring of 1948, Generals Walsh and Reckord and Bureau officials met for three hours one day and agreed to try for appropriations of $344,500,000 for the Guard—an increase of $164,500,000 over the amount approved by the Budget Bureau.[30] When issues came up within the administration of the Army, the Bureau chief often consulted the NGA before taking a position. For example, late in 1948 the secretary of the army was trying to get the Guard to agree to occupying armories jointly with the Reserves. General Walsh informed the Bureau chief that the Guard objected and that the NGA would support him in this stand.[31]

If the Bureau wanted to be successful it had to cooperate with the NGA, for it was the NGA that made the appeals to Congress for more appropriations, and it was the NGA's reputation for influence that made Army Department officials respond to the Bureau. A Bureau chief who dared to ignore the NGA would be ineffectual as a bureaucrat.

He might also be subject to serious embarrassment. Generals Cramer and Miltonberger discovered that it was costly to differ with the Association. In 1948 General Cramer was forced to accept a change in a major training directive that he had approved. General Miltonberger was chastised when, contrary to the position of the NGA, he asked Guard division commanders in 1946 to support a universal military training program of six months. General Walsh promptly telegraphed: (1) the secretary of war, condemning Miltonberger's action, (2) Miltonberger, demanding that he withdraw his telegram, (3) officials of the American Legion, the leading promoter of UMT, saying that the Guard's position was unchanged, and (4) Guard division commanders and adjutants general, telling them to ignore Miltonberger's request.[32]

The NGA was usually able to keep the Bureau chiefs in line, but there was little it could do to assure efficient, effective performance by the Bureau—and this above all was what the NGA wanted. The Association depended on the Bureau to carry out its administrative functions in such a way as to reflect credit upon the Guard. The Bureau chiefs were expected to be cogent and well-informed in their appearances before Congress, and to maintain an orderly, well-disciplined administration. The NGA therefore was extremely embarrassed in 1949 when a feud broke out in the Bureau. The conflict was between the chief, General Cramer, and Major General George Finch, an Air Guard officer who headed the Air Division. (In 1948 the Bureau had been organized into an Army Division and an Air Division with a Guard major general heading each.) After prolonged fighting with Finch, Cramer tried to relieve him. Cramer had insisted on handling all papers relating to Guard affairs. Finch and the Air Force charged that he did not handle them fairly. Cramer in turn charged that Finch deferred more to the Air Force than to him and made decisions behind his back. The NGA viewed the whole incident as a disgrace to the Guard and tried for a long time to avoid becoming involved. When the feud finally broke into the open, the NGA was concerned chiefly to protect the "integrity of the Bureau" against possible assaults by the Air Force. Generals Walsh and Reckord participated in several meetings with Army and Air Force officials at which the problem was discussed.[33]

Vis-à-vis top officials in the War Department and later the Army and Air Force departments, the NGA's tactics varied considerably with the personalities and issues involved. To some friendly officials—Secretary Patterson was one—the NGA had simply to appeal, much as it appealed to Congress, if it thought the Guard's interests were in danger. When the Guard was threatened with competition from the Reserves in 1946, Generals Walsh and Reckord agreed to demand a conference with the secretary of war, chief of staff, and other General Staff officers, but six days later General Reckord had dinner with the secretary of war and reached an understanding, making a major conference unnecessary.[34] Tougher tactics were used against the Air Force two years later. After conferring with Reckord and officers in the Bureau, General Walsh concluded in 1948 that "the Air Force might be forced to end its efforts [to get control over the Guard] if measures were introduced to abolish flying pay, temporary ranks and to press for an investigation of the sale of liquor at Bolling Field and other Air Installations." Some version of this threat was communicated then or later to Symington.[35] As this incident suggests, the NGA did not regard its political opponents in the Pentagon with awe or deference. General Reckord, in his imperious way, looked askance at "the young men in authority over the Air Force," as he once termed them.[36] To be sure, the Air Force was newer to Washington than General Reckord. He seems to have regarded it as an impudent upstart.

Whatever the NGA's tactics, its influence in the executive branch continued to depend fundamentally on its influence with Congress. Officials at the top of Army and Air Force administration responded to the NGA in the knowledge that Congress, which had final authority in the issues at stake, was on the Guard's side. This was evident especially in regard to the Gray Board report, with its recommendation for merging the Guard and the Reserves in a single federal reserve force. The Army never seriously contemplated trying to carry this out, for the proposal was widely recognized as a political anachronism. General Walsh noted receiving several letters from congressmen who condemned the report (spontaneously, it should be emphasized—the NGA did not solicit these letters). Representative Engel, chairman of the National Military Establishment Appropriations Subcommittee, wrote General Walsh that the report had as much chance of being carried out as a "snowball has of freezing in hell." [37] The Air Force did contemplate federalization, but gave the attempt up in 1949 after the President failed to join the effort and after the NGA had demonstrated that Congress would protect the Guard's dual status.

Success at one point stimulated success at another for the NGA. Each demonstration of congressional favor for the Guard encouraged concessions from the executive branch. In turn, the efficiency of the Guard's administrative operations increased its success with Congress. "The National Guard is always very dependable in doing what they say they will do," Representative Engel gratuitously observed to General Reckord in 1946.[38] The chief reason for this dependability was that money appropriated to the Bureau constituted money quickly available to the states for support of the Guard. Prodding from the NGA encouraged both the Bureau and Guard leaders in the states to act promptly in reorganizing Guard units. The Guard's image of dependability was carefully cultivated in congressional testimony by General Walsh, who persistently claimed with more zeal than accuracy that the Guard was meeting its strength goals.

The period of the Walsh-Reckord ascendancy demonstrates in extreme form the practical meaning of the Guard's autonomy. As the unchallenged leaders of the NGA, the two men embodied the interests of forty-eight states in the Guard and had access at the federal level to all points at which decisions importantly affecting the Guard were made. By their activity they linked these points into a simple, well-enclosed system, readily susceptible to their manipulation. To the extent that there was one locus of decision-making for Guard affairs, it was the NGA. The dispersed formal authority of decision-makers in Congress and the executive branch was to a large extent superseded by the concentrated, quasi-formal authority that Generals Walsh and Reckord accumulated and exercised. They directed an autonomous structure of power—an "empire within an empire," General Walsh liked to call it—transcending the federal-state, executive-legislative divisions of power that were contrived by the authors of the United States Constitution.

The NGA's quasi-formal authority was strikingly epitomized in the person of General Reckord. As the Guard's lobbyist, Reckord was highly successful in authoring policies for the Guard and exploiting them after they had been invested with official sanction by either the War Department or Congress. There was the case of the Guard's protective clause, which Congress enacted in 1940 and re-enacted in 1948. "Congress has declared," General Reckord would solemnly intone, "that the strength and organization of the National Guard shall be at all times maintained and assured." This was true enough, but the whole truth was that this declaration had been drafted by General Reckord himself and demanded as the price of Guard support for the selective service acts. Or he would cite the 1945 statement of War Department reserve policies that committed the federal government to providing armories for the Guard. "The War Department has stated . . . ," he would begin. Again, the whole truth was that the statement was Reckord's own work. General Reckord's various roles as author of policies for the Guard are hard to sort out, for the differences among them are subtle. When he supervised the drafting of postwar reserve policies in 1945, he was an officer of the Army of the United States on active duty. Subsequently he resumed his role as an official of the NGA, yet he retained in practice a degree of authority scarcely distinguishable from that of a War Department official though he had far more freedom of action.

In the fall of 1948, following major successes with respect to appropriations, retirement pay, and the Selective Service Act, General Walsh remarked to the NGA conference that "it is to be questioned if any organization has been so successful in the legislative field in so brief a period of time as the National Guard Association." [39] His was a prejudiced view, but it was nevertheless difficult to quarrel with. Among the House Armed Services Committee staff there were joking references to "100 Per Cent Reckord."

As of June 30, 1946, there were only four federally recognized Guard units, comprising thirteen officers and thirty-one enlisted men. Four years later, on the eve of the Korean war, the Guard included 369,489 men, organized in twenty-seven divisions, twenty regimental combat teams, and twenty-seven air groups. The Guard had been restored and its traditional status preserved. Much of the credit for this belonged to the National Guard Association.

The political record of the Guard in the years following World War II is imposing. Nonetheless, it seems less so when placed in perspective. The NGA's goals, after all, were not radical. The NGA was after "wherewithal," in General Walsh's happy phrase. In asking men, money, and material, the Guard was seeking only to retain the position it had held throughout the century as the Army's first-line reserve force. In opposing federalization by the Air Force, the Guard likewise was defending existing law and tradition as well as its own interests. This circumstance helps explain its success. The Guard's goals were essentially defensive. In advancing them the NGA had the advantage of speaking for a recognized interest group of long standing. When the NGA approached Congress or the executive branch, it did so with an acknowledged "right to speak" for an interest with an acknowledged "right to be heard."

These advantages, while enduring, have not been immutable. The immediate postwar years mark the apex of the NGA's success. During the cold war the political advantages of the Guard have declined.

CHAPTER V ✦ YEARS OF DEFENSE:
THE COLD WAR

The cold-war years have substantially altered the favorable political setting from which the Guard earlier benefited. The Guard's basic interests have been threatened repeatedly by environmental changes over which it has had no control. On the whole, the Guard has defended itself successfully, but this has required a major lobbying effort. The NGA had developed into a highly sophisticated organization.

THREATS TO THE GUARD

The Guard today, as always, seeks to preserve its constitutional freedom from federal control in peacetime and to maintain its traditional position as a combat reserve component. Both of these goals have been jeopardized by radical changes in United States military policy and institutions.

The Guard's autonomy has been challenged by a massive expansion of federal authority in military affairs. Before World War II, the function of maintaining military forces was to a significant extent shared by the federal government and the states. The National Guard was larger than the Army, and the states bore a substantial share of its cost. As of 1933, there were 130,000 men in the Army as compared with 185,000 in the National Guard, and the states were providing about one-third of the financial support for the Guard. Thirty years later, following the enormous growth of United States military force during the cold war, the role of the states in national defense was unimportant. The National Guard constituted a small portion of the total of United States military manpower. The active Army and Air Force included 1,934,000 men, the Army and Air Guard only 450,000. The states' share of support of the National

Guard had dwindled to about 6 percent. Armory maintenance and their share (25 percent) of the cost of new armories are the only substantial functions with respect to the Guard that remain a financial responsibility of the states.[1] Even though the federal government provides the Guard with a far larger share of its support and a larger amount of support than ever before, expenditures for the Guard have become a small share of total federal expenditures for military purposes. In 1933, when the federal government was paying only two-thirds of the cost of maintaining the Guard, federal expenditures for the Guard were over one-tenth of the War Department's entire budget for military purposes. As of 1963, when the federal share of Guard support was over 90 percent, expenditures for the Guard ($683,600,000) were only 4 percent of all Army and Air Force expenditures for personnel and operation and maintenance, and as a share of the total military budget, they were insignificant. The Guard, in brief, has been transformed from the largest military force in the country—in principle the mainstay of United States military strength—into a relatively small force, of peripheral significance.

The extension of federal authority in matters relating to the Guard is manifested not just in the growth of the professional services and in the size of the federal defense budget. It is manifested as well in the federal monopoly of the military manpower supply. The cold war began for the Guard when President Truman in 1948 responded to the Communist coup in Czechoslovakia by calling for universal military training and a new draft law. Though the Selective Service Act of 1948 protected the Guard by guaranteeing it a source of manpower, the act severely compromised the Guard's autonomy. Always before, recruits of the Guard had been unequivocally volunteers, enlisted by the states and offered to the federal government, albeit insistently, as a bonus to national defense. Since passage of the 1948 act, the Guard has depended on federal action to provide incentives for its recruits. Along with these incentives have come federally imposed conditions for recruitment that further reduce the Guard's freedom. The Guard has become the prisoner of federal military manpower policies.

The threats to the Guard are the result partly of institutional change. The National Security Act of 1947, by creating a single National Military Establishment headed by a secretary of defense, provided a mechanism for the increase of federal control over military affairs. Of much more importance has been the revolution in the nature of warfare. In turn, there has been a revolution in United States military strategy, and the Guard has sometimes seemed in danger of perishing in that revolution.

The Guard was in principle a mainstay of American military power when the basic American strategy was built around the concept of mobilization. This strategy, which prevailed before World War II, was based on the assumption that war would start elsewhere than on the American continent, and that the United States as a consequence would have time to prepare an adequate military force. The strategy required, among other things, a strong Navy to protect against invasion, a large organized reserve force (the National Guard), which could be mobilized in an emergency, and a strong civilian economy capable of rapid expansion for wartime production. Following World War II, this strategy was abandoned in favor of one built around the concept of deterrence. The change was impelled by changes in the structure of international politics (principally the development of Soviet-American rivalry) and in weapons technology (development of nuclear weapons and means of rapid delivery), which make it certain that in case of major war the United States will be immediately and totally engaged. The new United States strategy has stressed the maintenance of forces-in-being, especially bombers and missiles with sufficient nuclear capability to deter an attack upon the United States.[2] The problem facing the Guard, as an organization handed down from the era of mobilization and before, has been to secure a combat role within the framework of the new strategy. For the first time, heightened national need for military strength does not work automatically to the Guard's advantage.

The strategy of deterrence has posed two threats to the Guard. First, it has called into question the utility of ground forces in general, either in being or in reserve. The trend of United States military policy during the cold war has been to place heavy reliance on air and missile power at the expense of ground forces.[3] Insofar as this has been the case, the Guard has been no more threatened than the Army. Secondly, the strategy has placed a high premium on readiness, and has thereby called into question the utility of reserve forces in particular. During the cold war, the Guard has constantly been under pressure from the Defense Department to improve its readiness. More recently, it has been under pressure to reduce its size.

The Guard has been vulnerable to the charge of being unready, for Congress failed after the war to enact universal military training, which War Department planners had counted on to make it ready. The Korean war soon dramatized the issue. Within five days after the Communist invasion of South Korea, Congress hastily suspended the Guard's protective clause to allow the President to order all members and units of the reserve components to active duty.* First to be called were individual federal reservists, mostly veterans of World War II. Eight divisions, three regimental combat teams, and 714 company-size units of the Army Guard as well as two light bomber wings, nineteen fighter wings, and one tactical reconnaissance wing of the Air Guard were eventually mobilized, but it took seven to nine months to prepare the divisions for combat.[4] The war revealed how flimsy was the Guard's guarantee of a front-line role. Moreover, the war stimulated a Defense Department proposal for new reserve forces legislation—the Armed Forces Re-

---

* For the text of the Guard's protective clause, see page 58.

serve Act of 1952—the broad purpose of which was to improve the Reserves, the Guard's rival.

The next threat came during the early years of the Eisenhower Administration, when the New Look policy was being developed. For a time, defense policy planners contemplated converting the Guard into a home defense force. However, in the form enunciated, the New Look proved to be of benefit to the Guard. As a policy of heavy reliance on nuclear striking power, it involved a reduction in active Army forces and a compensatory increase in trained reserve forces. Following the New Look, the Guard was under welcome pressure from the Defense Department to increase its strength, and for a brief time it seemed to have a secure future if it could achieve a satisfactory level of readiness. In 1954 the Defense Department attacked the problem of reserve forces' readiness with a proposal for a six-months' training program for reservists, and Congress authorized such a program in the Reserve Forces Act of 1955, but did not require participation by Guard members. Men could belong to the Guard with only the training received in weekly drills and a two-week summer camp. The issue of Guard readiness came to a climax in 1957, when the Army, in a major extension of federal control over the Guard, directed that all of its recruits must take six months of active-duty training.

The Army's action seemed at last to settle the recurring issue of the Guard's readiness, but even so it was not the end of threats to the Guard's interests. Very shortly, the Defense Department abandoned the policy of increasing the size of reserve forces and instead sought to reduce them. Both the Eisenhower and Kennedy administrations proposed reductions in the number of Guard divisions and personnel. The Kennedy proposals followed a partial mobilization of reserve forces in the summer of 1961, which again called the readiness of the Guard into question.

These threats have occupied the NGA in the cold-war years.

It has been busy defending the Guard. Except for authorization of federal funds for armories, which Congress passed in 1950, the Guard has made no significant new demands upon the federal government since passage of the retirement bill in 1948. "All the Guard needs," General Reckord pleaded with Congress in 1951, "is to be let alone." [5] The plea was futile. In the dynamic environment of the cold-war years, the Guard's political goals have repeatedly been jeopardized. In addition, and apart from the cold war's threats, the burden of the Guard's political business has increased enormously. Guard affairs have become much more complicated. General Reckord, when reminded in 1960 of the nickname "100 Per Cent Reckord," replied nostalgically: "You know, it's true. It's hard to believe now but I used to go down there [Washington] and get a hundred per cent. Everything was simple then. You'd just draw up a bill and get it passed. But you can't do that now. Everything's complicated. All kinds of people get in the act. There's so much red tape." As the military establishment has grown, the number of official actions and rumors of official actions that concern the Guard has multiplied. The NGA has to deal with this burden.

CHANGE IN THE GUARD'S ENVIRONMENT:
THE DEFENSE BUREAUCRACY

Because of the increase of federal responsibility for the Guard, it is more important than ever for the NGA to be able to influence the administrative and policy-making activities within the executive branch. It is urgent that the Guard's administrative autonomy, which has been institutionalized in the National Guard Bureau, be protected. However, like other interests of the Guard, this one has been severely jeopardized. Under the impact of the cold war, an extensive bureaucracy has developed in the Defense Department. Authority for decisions affecting the Guard has been dispersed throughout a complex Pentagon hierarchy, culminating in the secretary of defense and, above him, in the National Security Council. This bureaucracy exercises a monopoly over the formulation and proposal of policies in the Guard's sphere of interest. It is not readily accessible to the Guard.

The Office of the Assistant Secretary of Defense (Manpower, Personnel, and Reserves), which was established in 1952, is the principal overseer of reserve forces policy. The Reserve Forces Policy Board, which was established in 1949 (as the Civilian Components Policy Board), also advises the secretary of defense on reserve policy. The Guard has four representatives among the Board's nineteen members, of whom reservists constitute a majority. In addition to these agencies, there are others in the Office of the Secretary of Defense that make decisions importantly affecting the Guard, especially the Office of the Comptroller. Decisions on strategy and force levels by the Joint Chiefs of Staff have an impact on the Guard. Within the Army and the Air Force, assistant secretaries had authority over manpower and reserve affairs for several years until the Kennedy Administration abolished these offices in 1961 and turned their responsibilities over to the service undersecretaries. Of most significance for the Guard, the Army and Air Force have each set up an assistant chief of staff for reserve components. These offices originated in 1948 when President Truman directed that a high-ranking regular officer be named to head the reserve program in each department. Beginning simply as "special assistants"—one-man offices for liaison between the reserves and administration of the regular services—they burgeoned into full-fledged staff operations. By 1956 the Army's special assistant was menacing the authority of the National Guard Bureau. For months the Bureau fought suggestions for a deputy chief of staff's office to which it would be subordinate. In the end, the assistant chief of staff was established with authority for planning the "major force, installation, and material objectives for the National Guard [and] the Army Reserve." A footnote to this regulation safeguarded to the Bureau (and to the chief, Army Reserve and ROTC affairs) "staff responsibility" for reserve programming under "coordination" of the assistant chief of staff.[6] The Bureau's authority remained largely intact.*

The Guard occasionally has sought to counteract the damaging effects of the new bureaucracy by placing its own representatives in administrative positions, but these efforts have not succeeded. In 1954 Colonel John L. Strauss, an Air Guard officer who later became the NGA's general counsel, tried for appointment as deputy assistant secretary of the Air Force for reserve and ROTC affairs. Late in 1956, General Walsh encouraged Major General Jim Dan Hill, commander of Wisconsin's 32d Division and president of Wisconsin State College, to become a candidate for assistant secretary of defense (manpower, personnel, and reserves). Hill had an interview with Secretary of Defense Charles E. Wilson, who made it plain that he was not

---

* The following statement in 1957 by Army Vice Chief of Staff Williston B. Palmer suggests the implications for the Guard of the assistant chief of staff's office: "There were two staff divisions, 'Reserve and ROTC Affairs' and the National Guard Bureau, each of which administered a separate element of the annual Army appropriation. It had become progressively more evident that, if we were ever going to relate our reserve components to JCS-approved programs for all forces, both active and reserve, necessary for the Army to make a single picture of its reserve component availabilities and capabilities, it could not be done effectively with two separate reserve programs, which historically were more closely related to the aspirations of the respective reserve components than to the strategic necessities of the United States.

"The creation of an Assistant Chief of Staff for Reserve Components amounted to removing the Special Assistant (for Civilian Components) from his ivory tower and giving him the necessary staff to take on a real, comprehensive, and continuing job of supervising a unified Reserve Components Program." (Letter, October 25, 1957, to Charles Dale Story, cited in Story, "The Formulation of Army Reserve Forces Policy: Its Setting Amidst Pressure Group Activity," unpub. diss., University of Oklahoma, 1958, p. 179).

According to Pentagon sources, the assistant chief of staff's office has not had the impact that Palmer's letter implies. In practice, its principal effect has been to help provide the Army Reserve with the wherewithal that for years has been supplied to the Guard by the Bureau acting in concert with the NGA.

under consideration for the vacancy. Under General Walsh, the NGA sometimes considered the possibility of forcing from office persons believed unfriendly to the Guard. In 1950 Walsh participated with Senators Edward J. Thye, Joseph R. McCarthy, Bourke B. Hickenlooper, George Aiken, and John W. Bricker in a meeting at which the suitability of Mrs. Anna M. Rosenberg to be assistant secretary of defense for manpower was discussed. Walsh suspected Mrs. Rosenberg of being hostile to the Guard as a result of her conduct in office following a recess appointment. Senator McCarthy, at least, suspected her of being a communist sympathizer. The Senate confirmed Mrs. Rosenberg.

Not only has the NGA been hampered by development of new administrative authorities. It has also suffered from the reduced accessibility of authority long established. No longer can the chief of the National Guard Bureau or the president of the NGA obtain casual entry to the office of the Army chief of staff or other leading officials. These officials have become busy men.

The National Guard Bureau and Guard members of the Section Five committees in the Army and Air Force continue to serve as spokesmen for the Guard within the Defense Department and as sources of information for the NGA, but they have often been excluded from serious consideration of reserve policy. The Section Five committees, which in 1945 were intended to be the source of policies governing the Guard, have become anachronistic in a time when defense policy-making is a complex, continuing process. They meet only four times a year for a little more than a day. Furthermore, because the regular, Reserve, and Guard panels normally meet together, the seven Guard members can easily be outvoted by a coalition of fourteen regulars and Reserves.

The effect of these developments has been to destroy permanently the simple, accessible system of decision-making for Guard affairs that was described in the previous chapter. NGA influence on the executive is limited. Policy initiatives have become virtually impossible for the Guard. In the interest of its own independence, if for no other reason, the newly built reserve forces bureaucracy cannot accept the NGA's proposals. Any major proposal that bears the stamp of NGA origin is almost certain to be rejected in the Pentagon, whatever its intrinsic merits. The NGA can submit minor pieces of legislation directly to Congress, but these are routinely referred to the Defense Department for comment, and they are often long delayed or killed in the process. Nor does the NGA find it easy to influence policy planning within the executive branch. Its difficulties are illustrated by the Pentagon's handling of the Armed Forces Reserve Act of 1952, the National Reserve Plan of 1954, and the Army's six-months' training directive of 1957, matters of major interest to the Guard.

The Armed Forces Reserve Act was prepared by the Reserve Forces Policy Board. The NGA president testified before the Board, and Guard representatives on the Board kept the NGA informed. Still, the Guard was a remote participant in the formulation process. It participated even less during 1953 and 1954 in formulation of the National Reserve Plan (foundation of the Reserve Forces Act of 1955). This was prepared by the National Security Training Commission (a statutory citizens' commission established in 1951 and abolished six years later), the Office of Defense Mobilization, the National Security Council, and within the Defense Department, *ad hoc* committees more than the Reserve Forces Policy Board. The training directive originated in a memorandum from the secretary of defense to the service secretaries directing that after April 1, 1957, all reserve recruits must receive at least four months' basic training. In response to the memorandum, the Army Staff developed plans for an uninterrupted six-month period of training. The National Guard Bureau asked for one or two three-month periods, to prevent interruption of the school year. The chief of staff decided on the six-month plan. After he made this decision, the

plan was submitted to the Section Five Committee, meeting
with regular, Reserve, and Guard members, who approved it
thirteen to seven. The regulars and Reserves voted solidly for
it, the Guard solidly against. The Army then sent its six-months'
training plan to the secretary of defense, who approved it.[7]

The Guard's exclusion from direct participation in policy
planning does not mean that its interests are not considered and
its reaction anticipated. The National Reserve Plan would
probably have called for converting the Guard into a home-
defense force except that planners anticipated that Guard opposition would kill such a proposal in Congress. Besides, the
interests and objectives of the many new Defense Department
agencies with a share of control over Guard matters do not
invariably conflict with those of the Guard. The agencies that
administer reserve affairs seek to sustain the reserve forces;
typically, they clash with the Guard over issues of federal control, but they are partisans of the Guard within the Defense
Department in its struggle to maintain strength.

Nevertheless, any major proposal that comes from the Defense
Department is likely to contain much that the Guard objects to,
and the NGA is forced to fight its battles in Congress. The
Guard's dependence on Congress, always heavy, is now virtually complete. In its relations with the Pentagon, the NGA is
increasingly limited to gathering intelligence so that it may plan
countermeasures on Capitol Hill.

CHANGE IN THE GUARD'S ENVIRONMENT:
CONGRESS AND THE RESERVES

Frustrated by the decreasing accessibility of the Defense
Department, the NGA has had to look for help to its traditional
ally, Congress, but even there changes detrimental to the Guard
have taken place.

The problem is not that Congress' attitude toward the Guard
has changed. On the contrary, to a remarkable degree the

Guard retains its traditional appeal to Congress as a citizen soldiery with a foundation in the state governments. Despite the decline of antimilitarist sentiment, which has become anachronistic in contemporary United States society, as late as 1962 a Defense Appropriations Subcommittee member could appeal for a strong Guard on the following grounds:

. . . we have in mind that we do not wish ever to turn the Nation over to a military clique, and that we do not ever wish to take the position that only West Point, the Naval Academy, and the Air Force Academy can furnish officers competent to lead the Armed Forces in time of war.[8]

Similarly, members of Congress still pay homage to the Guard as a symbol of states' rights, although the concept that a state militia should safeguard civil liberties by checking the professional army's power is now only quaint constitutional lore.[9] One congressman declared in 1960:

And I am convinced that "there are they" in this country who don't believe we need it [the Guard]. And we who know that it is needed have got to protect it on a long-range basis. . . . It is the only army our States have. It is the only modus whereby order can be restored in an emergency and calamities and disasters treated with. And unless we have a Guard, we just don't have a country. That is the thing that makes up the part of the whole—the entities of the States. And I don't ever want to see the day when the percentage of those who don't believe in the States will be greater than those who do.[10]

Not surprisingly, the congressman who said this was a South Carolinian, but Northerners too continue to respect the Guard as a vehicle for dispersion of power. In an interview in 1959, a newly retired congressional veteran, John M. Vorys of Ohio, declared, "I always gave the Guard the benefit of the doubt because I figure that too much centralization of power is a bad thing."[11]

The number of congressmen who are or have been members of the Guard is less than formerly (recent congresses have con-

tained fewer than six, and none so prominently identified with
the Guard as was Senator Martin). Yet the Guard continues to
enjoy easy access to numerous congressmen and to have strong
ties to a few, principally ex-governors and Southerners. As of
1953 Senator Saltonstall was linked to the Guard in the following ways. The chief of the National Guard Bureau, Major General Edgar C. Erickson, had served as Massachusetts adjutant
general when Saltonstall was governor and had been appointed
chief with Saltonstall's backing. Major General Edward D. Sirois
of Lawrence, Massachusetts, who had been Republican floor
leader in the Massachusetts House in 1935–36 when Saltonstall
was speaker and who later was Saltonstall's campaign manager,
was commander of the 26th Division of Massachusetts and an
officer of the National Guard Association. The head of the NGA
staff, General Galusha, a native of Massachusetts, had served
Saltonstall in the state government as commissioner of agriculture and as assistant secretary to the governor, and in the federal
government as a member of the Senate Armed Services Committee staff. Finally, Saltonstall knew routinely the adjutant
general of Massachusetts, as any senator would know the adjutant general of his state.

The difficulty for the Guard arises partly over the circumstance
that congressmen, like top officials in the executive branch, are
far busier than they used to be. They handle a great deal of
military legislation, and it has become harder to get their attention for Guard matters. A more serious difficulty is Congress'
increasing responsiveness to the Reserves. As the Reserves have
grown in number, they have become an important constituent
group. Many members of Congress (forty-seven in the 86th
Congress, according to biographical entries in the *Congressional
Directory*) are Reserve officers. No longer does congressional
suspicion of federal military power restrain growth of a federal
reserve, as it did for many years. This suspicion, at least in
regard to the Reserves, has disappeared under the impact of the

cold war. The Reserves have come to be regarded as a legitimate interest, to be protected and preserved as is the Guard. Congress is concerned to give the two rival reserve forces equal treatment. This attitude has been beneficial to the Reserves and detrimental to the Guard, whose advantage over the Reserves has been narrowed by congressional action. When the NGA persuades Congress to take action in the Guard's favor, Congress often extends the favor to the Reserves. They have more than once ridden the Guard's coattails to political success.

Since passage of the Reserve Forces Act of 1955 the Reserves' position has improved substantially in relation to that of the Guard. In 1954 only 127,160 Army Reservists were receiving armory drill pay, compared to 282,962 men for the Army Guard. By 1960 Army Reserve paid drill strength had jumped to 300,000, while that for the Army Guard was 400,000. Reserve personnel appropriations in Fiscal Year 1963 were $289,300,000, not much less than the Guard personnel appropriation of $314,800,000. Since 1956 all Reserve units in the "ready reserve" have held forty-eight armory drills a year, the same as the Guard. The Guard retains mobilization priority over the Reserves and in general its units are better equipped. Growth of a competitor has nonetheless compounded the cold war's perils to the Guard, primarily by increasing pressure to yield to federal control. If the Guard does not do what the Defense Department wants, it runs the risk of losing out to the Reserves.

DEVELOPMENT OF THE NGA

To cope with its political problems, the Guard maintains a high level of political activity. The NGA probably comes as close to organizational perfection as a lobby can. No longer does it depend simply on the dynamism of one or two leaders. It is a highly rationalized structure. The case of the Guard in the cold-war years is therefore useful for assessing the efficacy of a well organized lobby.

Since 1953 the NGA has regularly enrolled virtually 100

percent of its potential membership, a total usually of about 47,000 officers. This remarkable performance results from the military character of the organization: dues are collected through the command structure. Major General Leo M. Boyle, adjutant general of Illinois and membership chairman of the NGA, explained this technique to the adjutants general in 1952:

> We ask that you also try to impress upon your commanding officers of the units, from the company on up, to get them to get behind the membership for early collection. . . . That is what we do in Illinois. It is a man's responsibility, as far as we are concerned, and each commander accepts that responsibility, and dues are collected and they are mailed in. . . . It is a very simple problem if you just do it that way.

General Boyle went on to explain a technique that has become standard in the Guard—requiring payment of NGA dues with the application for a commission:

> . . . it is S. O. P. with us in Illinois, that when the 2d Lieutenant's papers come in for consideration by the Adjutant General for appointment—he has certain papers and forms that must be there, and one of those forms is a check with his application for membership in the National Guard Association. Now, Gentlemen, it works.[12]

In 1959 the NGA raised dues to $7, $10, and $20. Not only are all active Guard officers expected to join, but retired ones are organized in an "Old Guard" to increase the leverage of the Association and guarantee continuity in case of mobilization.

The day-to-day activities of the NGA are in the hands of an able and well-paid professional staff. In all, a staff of approximately twenty-five employees draws an annual payroll of $125,000. They have been housed since 1959 at the foot of Capitol Hill in a two-million-dollar headquarters that was financed by contributions from the membership. In 1960 the NGA had assets of over $2.6 million. Its annual expenditures reached $464,500 in 1957, compared with $62,519 in 1948 and $198,000 in 1952.

To some extent growth of the NGA during the cold war

represents the natural evolution of the organization that General Walsh launched in 1944–46. Walsh planned development of a staff at the beginning of his presidency. He then added new members as the organization acquired a stable income. Beyond that, it is clear that the added political burdens of the cold war made expansion of the NGA necessary. In 1949, in response to controversy over the Gray Board report, Walsh retired as adjutant general of Minnesota and began to spend full time at NGA headquarters. General Reckord's activity in the NGA began to diminish soon after that, and only by drawing heavily on personnel in the National Guard Bureau, several of whom were temporarily assigned to assist the NGA, was General Walsh able to handle the problems that preceded passage of the Armed Forces Reserve Act of 1952. Following this demonstration of its acute need for professional help, the Association hired a legislative agent. Two years later, following the Reserve Forces Act of 1955, it hired a general counsel (the legislative agent then became executive assistant to the NGA president). In 1958, following the active-duty training controversy with the Army, the NGA hired a public relations man.

General Walsh remained as president of the NGA until 1957, when he retired in favor of a hand-picked successor, Major General William H. Harrison, Jr., of Massachusetts. The change seems to have come when Walsh sensed that the Association wanted a more tractable leadership. There is evidence of dissent from Walsh's dogmatism in the last years of his presidency. Late in 1955, the Defense Department ordered that Guard recruits who volunteered for six-months' training should serve in a federal status rather than in their status as militia. General Walsh publicly announced that the NGA would fight the order as a violation of the militia clause, but lack of support within the NGA forced him to retreat. Early in 1956 he wrote in his diary:

Met with General Harrison and advised him that it had become increasingly evident that there was a rather sharp divergence in the thinking of the Association and the President in connection with RFA 55 and other areas. Also, that it appeared the Association was committing itself to a policy of placation and appeasement instead of fighting for principles and carrying the war into Africa.

The transfer of power from General Walsh's generation of officers to the next was associated with a gradual increase in professionalism among Guard officers. The use of Guard officer appointments as patronage has sharply declined in the cold-war years. It has not been abandoned entirely. In many states a change in control of the governor's office may be followed by a change in the office of adjutant general. (General Harrison himself was replaced as adjutant general of Massachusetts by an outgoing Democratic governor in 1960.) The patronage tradition continues to flourish in a few states in the Deep South.[13] Otherwise, the Guard's links to party politics are disintegrating. The military analyst of the *New York Times,* Hanson Baldwin, observed in 1962 that "On the whole, National Guard officers today are probably more highly qualified professionally than the Reserve officers of most, if not all, other nations on earth." [14] No longer redolent of state and local politics, today's Guard is oriented as much to the Pentagon as to the county courthouse. The change is doubtless symptomatic of a general change in the structure of American politics.

As the character of the Guard has changed, so has the style of the NGA. The dogmatic hostility to the professional services has abated. Though bold, the NGA is no longer so combative as when Walsh and Reckord were its leaders. The change in the NGA's style is evident especially in the professional staff. These men are acute and articulate, with personal styles of behavior and speech that suggest the professional armed services, the upper ranks of the federal civil service, or corporate business. Of the three members, one came to the NGA from the staff of the Senate Armed Services Committee, and two came following several years' service in the Pentagon as Guard officers on active duty.* On the tables in Association headquarters, amid a setting of ultramodern decor, are journals as worldly as *The Reporter* and *Orbis*. Through its carpeted suites move shades of bankers' grey. Whereas General Walsh was fiery and impassioned, the current staff, though unequivocally loyal to the Guard, are detached and dispassionate. Whereas General Walsh disliked the Pentagon to the point of disgust, the NGA's general counsel spends more time there than on Capitol Hill. In summary, to cope with the problems raised by the growth of the Defense Department bureaucracy, the Guard has hired bureaucrats of its own—men who have worked in the offices of official Washington and who possess skills that enable them to communicate with others who still work there.

In the hands of this staff, development and exploitation of the Guard's resources of political influence have become conscious, methodical processes. In part, the NGA has simply practiced traditional techniques with new sophistication. In part, it has developed additional ones.

THE NGA'S TECHNIQUES

Pressure.   Basically, the NGA relies now, as always, on communications to congressmen from Guard members in their districts. This kind of appeal for help will be called "pressure." The word is put in quotation marks to warn that it is misleading. The function of the Guard's grass-roots messages to Congress is not to force action under threat of a penalty. It is to alert congressmen that the Guard has an interest in an impend-

---

* In 1950, at the request of the Army and the NGA, Congress provided that 40 percent of the officers on duty in the National Guard Bureau should be Guardsmen. These slots and those of the resident members of the Section Five committees enable a sizable number of Guard officers to acquire administrative experience in the Pentagon. In recruiting a staff, the NGA has drawn from this group.

ing issue, and to activate their latent predispositions in favor of the Guard.

On account of the presence of a full-time staff at NGA headquarters, the NGA today uses pressure more skillfully and systematically than ever before. Proximity to Capitol Hill makes it possible for NGA headquarters to perceive instantly when messages from the grass roots are needed. The convenience of today's telephone facilities makes it possible to stimulate such messages promptly and with certainty that they will be sent.

The NGA uses this technique selectively. It does not ordinarily sponsor mass telegram or letter-writing campaigns. Rather, it applies pressure on a few congressmen who have authority over Guard matters (members of the Armed Services committees or Defense Appropriations subcommittees) when an important vote is approaching. It stimulates messages from home-state friends of the congressmen whom it seeks to influence.

The same habit of approaching congressmen through their friends and neighbors is illustrated by the NGA's behavior at congressional hearings. Guard spokesmen are selected with an eye to composition of the committee. States represented on the committee are frequently represented on the witness stand, although care is taken that only the more competent officers appear. This technique, though transparent, does not offend committee members; they encourage it. Congressmen hearing Guard testimony may inquire after their adjutants general. "Where's Tony Biddle?" Representative Daniel J. Flood of Pennsylvania asked in 1956, referring to Adjutant General Anthony J. Drexel Biddle.[15] A committee chairman who has scheduled a hearing at which the Guard will appear may invite the adjutant general from his home state to be there.

Again, the technique of confronting congressmen with their

friends from home is not new, but it is practiced now with more system and deliberation, and, significantly, it has continued despite development of the professional staff. They rarely appear as witnesses before Congress. Instead, they defer to adjutants general and other leading Guard officers.

Some officials at NGA headquarters have maintained ties of friendship with congressmen, and these ties facilitate the NGA's appeals to Congress. This was especially true while General Walsh was active as NGA president. He made a daily habit of a walk across the Capitol Plaza for a few minutes' conversation on the Hill. Many members of Congress regarded him as a personal friend.[16] His successor, General Harrison, did not continue this practice, even after he retired as adjutant general of Massachusetts in 1960 and began to spend full time at NGA headquarters. A shy man, he was little known on Capitol Hill. According to several congressional sources, the change of leaders diminished the NGA's effectiveness there. The NGA's personal contacts were partially sustained, however, by the head of the professional staff, Brigadier General Mark H. Galusha, who knew a number of senators and committee staff members as a result of having served with the Senate Armed Services Committee from 1947 to 1953.*

In recent years, the NGA has exploited one imposing source of grass-roots strength for the first time. Despite its foundation in the states the Guard had never, before 1958, received much organized help from the governors. In 1958 threatened cuts in both the unit and numerical strength of the Guard brought the governors to its defense. A delegation of governors testified on behalf of the Guard before the House Armed Services Committee. The Governors' Conference passed resolutions supporting the Guard and set up a special committee which lobbied for it on Capitol Hill. When the NGA asked the Senate Defense

* In 1964 Major General James F. Cantwell of New Jersey succeeded General Harrison as president of the NGA, and General Galusha retired.

Appropriations Subcommittee to require the Defense Department to maintain the Army Guard at 400,000 men, within two days thirty-six governors sent telegrams to the subcommittee supporting the request. The governors' committee on the Guard has remained in existence, a convenient source of help to the NGA and an outlet for its propaganda. (The chairman for several years was S. Ernest Vandiver of Georgia, a former adjutant general.) All of the governors' activity has of course been stimulated by the NGA.[17]

Although NGA headquarters usually applies pressure selectively, carefully choosing both the sources of pressure and the objects of it, Guard members at the grass roots are not so discriminating. Whenever the Guard is faced with a political threat, a rash of letters and telegrams from officers and enlisted men appears in the *Congressional Record*. These are not necessarily sent to congressmen with authority in Guard matters, but go to members in general. Typically, they are stimulated by a zealous Guard officer on the local level. In 1962 a flood of messages from Texas protested cuts in the Guard. These came from city and county governments, chambers of commerce, and other local organizations, as well as Guard units. They had been stimulated by a major in the Texas National Guard who was ambitious for office in the National Guard Association.

NGA headquarters avoids sponsoring such campaigns because it knows that congressmen ignore or resent what is obviously staged. Anyway it is usually seeking to influence only a very few members of Congress. Issues of concern to the Guard rarely come to a vote on the floor. Nevertheless, locally inspired messages sent to congressmen at random may serve the NGA's purposes. The congressmen who receive such messages often insert them into the *Record* or forward them to the Armed Services or Appropriations committees for insertion into hearings. Sometimes congressmen who are under pressure from the Guard testify in its favor before the Armed Services or

Appropriations committees. In 1958 members from Utah, South Dakota, North Dakota, Georgia, Maine, Minnesota, and New York (Brooklyn), representing both rural and urban constituencies, wrote the House Defense Appropriations Subcommittee or appeared before it in support of a 400,000-man Guard. In 1962, when the Guard was again threatened with cuts, congressmen from twenty-one states defended it on the floor. The random, grass-roots messages probably have the effect, although indirectly, of heightening the awareness of key committee members that the Guard's interests are at stake in some matter —and this is precisely the objective of the NGA in stimulating pressure selectively.

Although the NGA does not arrange mass campaigns of pressure, it does seek whenever a political issue arises to coordinate the opinions and actions of the leading Guard officers. In 1957, when the issue over six-months' training arose, all of the adjutants general and division commanders were summoned to Washington to hear General Walsh urge united action. Similarly, at the peak of the fight over sustaining Guard strength in the summer of 1958, all of the adjutants general met together in Washington. All NGA members receive *The National Guardsman* and approximately 1500 officers attend the NGA's annual conferences. There the Association's leaders seek to stir their pride in the Guard's cohesiveness. As the NGA president put it in 1958: "Despite the fact that the membership of this Association represents widely divergent geographical areas and interests; despite the fact that we are a heterogeneous political group, we have successfully, and with exceptional singleness of purpose, unified ourselves for the enhancement of the common good." [18]

The NGA's efforts to coordinate action with respect to specific issues have usually been successful. Although the Walsh-Reckord generation of Guard officers, with its fierce hostility to the professional services, has passed from leadership, its successors continue to show strong loyalty to the Guard. Guardsmen have a reputation for being clannish. "They stick together," many sources agree. A veteran congressional committee staff member, asked in 1960 if support from the American Legion were of help to the Guard, replied that the Guard, being the better organized, does not need help. "Legion members don't even know what their national convention resolves," he said. "That doesn't happen with the Guard." This cohesive quality probably derives now, as earlier, from the military character of the Guard organization, and it is today powerfully reinforced in political matters by an habitually defensive posture. NGA leaders (General Harrison no less than General Walsh) denounce even the mildest of Pentagon moves as attempts to "destroy us." The undeniable threats to the Guard from the Defense Department give credence to such rhetoric. Impending martyrdom has become the Guard's normal state.

Altogether, the pressures generated by the Guard usually create the impression of a highly motivated group with strongly felt interests. There is a characteristic *élan* to the Guard's political activity that is the envy of other groups. The Guard is bold and audible. It speaks often and with conviction. The following letter from an enlisted man in Pennsylvania to his congressman is typical. The writer was protesting a proposal of the Defense Department in 1962 to abolish his unit:

Just think (not only of me) but the other boys in the 876 Company that have been putting in their time to serve their State and country and what it would mean to most all of us. If this unnecessary idea goes through think of the things that it will mean to our town of Indiana, our county, our State, as well.

Please do what I am willing to do and keep a good Company 876 active in Indiana. Really consider this matter before acting because it is really something important to us, Company D, 876.

Please do all you can in keeping us here in Indiana as 876.[19]

This capacity to communicate with Congress is the Guard's

principal resource of influence. "Well, they are never backward about letting us hear from them," Senator Saltonstall explained in answer to a question about the Guard's success with Congress.[20] When Representative Overton Brooks urged the House in 1958 to pass a resolution endorsing a 400,000-man Army Guard, he explained to the members: "We have inquiries now from some of the governors and the adjutants general. They were up here last week. They had a big meeting. We heard from them." [21] In 1962, in defense of the Guard's size, Senator John Sherman Cooper acknowledged that "men in these units write us and wish to have the units maintained. I shall not say that does not have any influence." [22]

The effect of these messages is not to force unwelcome action on reluctant congressmen. Rather, it is to draw their attention to issues of importance to the Guard. "They're so busy they can't keep track of what's going on," General Galusha observed. The function of the NGA is to tell them. Once they are made aware that the Guard feels an issue is important, they give support willingly. "You might say that Congress is prejudiced in favor of the National Guard," declared Senator Saltonstall. "I have never asked for a vote," General Galusha said in 1960. "I don't have to." General Reckord recalled, "I never tried to be close to them [members of Congress]. They're all good fellows. They always wanted to do the right thing." Some members of Congress are so sympathetic to the Guard that they appear positively grateful for being pressured. In hearings of a House Armed Services subcommittee in 1962, a veteran member told the president of the NGA: ". . . we know your position. You know ours. We are behind your efforts. And had it not been for the National Guard Association over the years, as well as at present, I don't know what the plight of the Guard would be." [23]

Information. A capacity to communicate useful information

to Congress is another important asset of influence for the Guard. "Information" differs from "pressure" in that it does not convey an explicit appeal for help. It is a report on an existing state of affairs.

The Guard's capacity to provide information depends upon the professional staff at NGA headquarters. One of their principal functions is to maintain contact with sources in the Defense Department (usually the National Guard Bureau) who can tell them of decisions or proposals impending in the Guard's sphere of interest. They also keep in touch with Guard leaders in the states, who tell them what the effects of Defense Department action or inaction are.

Internal communication is easy for the Guard. Of the 47,000 members of the NGA, fewer than 200 are general officers, who constitute the leadership elite. These men know one another from attendance at NGA conferences, membership on the Section Five committees, or service on the NGA Executive Council and standing committees. Between a third and a fourth of these general officers are adjutants general, who hold their own annual convention. There is a steady flow of sympathetic communication between Association headquarters and Guard leaders in the Bureau, Section Five committees, Reserve Forces Policy Board, and the state capitols. In particular, the Bureau chief and the NGA president communicate freely with each other (though the character of this communication varies with the personalities of the incumbents). When asked about his relations with the NGA, the Bureau chief in 1960, Major General Donald W. McGowan, replied exuberantly: "Just like that [holding up two intertwined fingers and slamming the table with the other hand for emphasis]. Why, Bill Harrison [the NGA president] and I grew up together." He meant that they grew up together in the Guard.[24]

Through this internal network, NGA headquarters keeps abreast of Guard affairs such as administration of the six-months' training program, deliveries of equipment, and the status of armory construction projects. When transmitted to Capitol Hill, this information helps Congress to legislate or to make pointed, relevant inquiries of executive officials. If the NGA's goal is to forestall unfavorable action by the executive branch, information transmitted to Congress may stimulate complaints which discourage the action. At the least, such information serves as a first alert to Congress that an issue which involves the Guard's interests is in the making. Congress cannot be moved to action in an instant, and the sooner an alert can be sounded, the better are the Guard's chances of success. Information lays the ground for an appeal for help (pressure).

Information, like pressure, is effective as a resource of influence because Congress is predisposed to help the Guard. A congressman who is told that construction of an armory in his district is being delayed because the Budget Bureau will not release the funds knows what to do with this information. The NGA does not have to ask that he call the Budget Bureau or the Army Department. Chances are that he will do so of his own accord.

Information of this kind enables the congressman to fulfill his various roles as lawmaker, critic of the executive branch, and representative of his constituents. Usually he cannot get such information from his staff (which does not have it or the time and expertise to seek it) or from the executive branch (which rarely provides information quickly and in convenient, readily comprehensible form). In any case, to solicit information is too much trouble for the congressman, a busy man with little time to spare, even if, as is unlikely, he knows precisely what questions to ask. The lobby becomes an important source of help.

The NGA is especially valuable to Congress in this respect because the Guard's sphere of interest, defense policy, is increasingly dominated by the executive branch. The Defense

Department monopolizes the supply of information, and Congress has difficulty reaching independent judgments without an independent supply of facts. The Guard and NGA, not being subject to control by the Defense Department, give Congress information with which to challenge the judgment of the Defense Department in reserve matters. This is illustrated by the following complaint of Representative Porter Hardy to the secretary of defense in 1959. Questioning the secretary on the basis of data from the NGA, Hardy declared, "That is the only way we can get a basis on which to ask you people questions, because you don't give us anything except what supports your position." [25] That the Guard's independence of the Defense Department serves the interests of Congress is one reason why Congress continues to protect that independence. [26]

Having a convenient source of information is especially valuable for congressmen in the case of a group, such as the Guard, which is dispersed throughout the country. "It would be an awful burden if we had to deal with all fifty states," according to the counsel of the House Armed Services Committee. [27] The NGA helps congressmen by serving as a clearing house and coordinator for communications from the entire Guard organization. (This is as true for communications of "pressure" as for those of "information.") The NGA also serves congressmen by supplying them with information about their hometown Guard units. In 1962 the head of the NGA's professional staff estimated that he gets up to 150 calls a year from the offices of congressmen who want to include a paragraph or two about the Guard in a speech to constituents. The NGA, after a call to the National Guard Bureau, supplies names of units, something of their combat history, and names of officers.

Reputation for Influence. The NGA's reputation as a powerful lobby is an important resource of influence. One of the principal tasks of the NGA staff is to preserve this reputation so that it will continue to be of use. This asset is of more value vis-à-vis the executive branch than Congress, although it may have some effect on Capitol Hill too.

The impression that the National Guard always gets what it wants is widespread in Washington. It tends to discourage the Guard's opponents. If they assume that the Guard is bound to win, they never even begin to fight. This appears to have happened in 1953–54, when the Defense Department failed to propose converting the Guard into a home defense force despite strong support for the proposal within the Defense Department. When rumors of the plan reached the NGA, General Walsh warned in a speech that "If they want war, let it begin here." [28] Two weeks later the assistant secretary of defense for manpower invited Walsh to the Pentagon to assure him that the Guard would not be relegated to a home defense role. The Guard's reputation for influence later inhibited an effort by the Eisenhower Administration to dissuade Congress from requiring maintenance of the Army Guard at 400,000 men. The effort, according to one of Eisenhower's congressional liaison men, was judged "not worth the carnage." [29]

The NGA's technique of exploiting its reputation for influence is illustrated by the following excerpts from a plan of action developed during the six-months' training controversy. Passages that are particularly relevant are italicized:

Recent actions and proposals by the Department of Defense make it clear that the Department is prepared to make a final and determined effort to reduce the National Guard in strength and relegate it to a secondary position in the military reserve establishment. The most critical proposal, that which would make six months active duty training a condition of National Guard enlistment, is now awaiting approval of the Secretary of Defense. While the National Guard is willing and anxious to accept a workable plan to increase the mobilization readiness of its units, it does not feel that the six months program can be successful and, if it is imposed on the Army National Guard, the result will be a drastic reduction in strength in the next year.

It is apparent that the Department of Defense is of a mind to test the political strength of the National Guard Association of the United States and force through its proposals, and thereby reduce the strength and effectiveness of the Army National Guard. Aware, as we are, that the Department of Defense is determined to put into effect these proposals despite the opposition of the National Guard of the United States, it is imperative that the Association take immediate and constructive action in two areas—legislative (political) action; and public relations. Purpose of this action is to force re-consideration of the six months proposal, or to delay finalizing the proposal until Congressional appeal may be made to protect the status of the Army National Guard. It is recommended that the following actions be taken by the National Guard Association and the Adjutants General Association:

a. [That] a statement be issued immediately by General Walsh, citing the effect of the proposal on the Army National Guard, expressing the concern of the entire National Guard over the proposal, and *announcing that an emergency meeting of Adjutants General and senior Guard Commanders will be held in Washington* on January 23, 1957, to consider implications of the proposal.

b. That the Adjutants General and Division Commanders be briefed at a session at Old Point Comfort on the night of January 22nd by General Jones, on armory construction problems, and by General Sage on the training and recruiting problems.

c. That the same group come to Washington on January 23rd for an emergency meeting, *to be given the widest possible publicity.*

d. That following the morning meeting on January 23rd, the individual General Officers contact their various Congressional representatives and express to them their grave concern over the future of the Guard and prompt a flood of inquiries by Members of the Congress to the Department of the Army and Department of Defense.

e. That immediately a number of key Governors wire key officials in the Executive Branch of the Government, expressing concern and requesting explanations and assurance that finalizing proposals affecting the Army National Guard will be delayed for further study.

f. That continued inquiries from Congressional, State and community sources be made regarding specific armory projects.

g. That the National Guard Association institute and continue an aggressive political action and public relations campaign, in a determined effort to protect the status of the Army National Guard.

h. [That] a letter [be sent] from General Walsh to each member of

Congress, citing the concern of the National Guard over the proposed six months training restriction.

    i. [That] a Senator and Representative rise in the Congress and call attention to the concern of the National Guard over the effect of the proposed Department of Defense action.[30]

When this plan was drawn up, the Army had not yet issued the training directive. The immediate objective of the NGA was to discourage it from doing so. The actions proposed in the plan were intended to warn the Army that the Guard was mobilizing its renowned political force, in the hope that the Army would retreat of its own accord. The actions were undertaken not because they were expected in themselves to have an effect, but because knowledge of them was expected to inhibit the Army.

When the technique failed (the Army issued the directive anyway), it became especially important for the NGA to find some other way of demonstrating its influence. The magnitude of the ensuing controversy suggests that the NGA's ability to get its way was more importantly at stake than the substance of the disagreement. (The controversy was ostensibly fought over the narrow issue of whether six months' training would be required of Guard recruits who were between the ages of seventeen and eighteen-and-a-half. For them alone the NGA sought an eleven-week program.) "We are going to have to decide," the assistant secretary of defense for manpower declared at the peak of the fight, "who determines what is necessary to meet military requirements—the Defense Department or the National Guard."[31] The NGA likewise viewed the fight as a crucial test of its influence. Should the directive be passively accepted, General Walsh warned the adjutants general and division commanders, "with it should come the realization that forevermore the Army Guard will accept whatever the Department of the Army ordains and the states, National Guard Bureau, and Section 5 Committee will become nonentities and might just as well cease to exist."[32]

In the end, the Army agreed under pressure from Congress to delay the training requirement for nine months. Though the central issue was compromised, the NGA had demonstrated the ability to make the Army retreat from its directive.

One important effect of the NGA's reputation for influence is to facilitate the Army's support for the Guard on issues which ally the two. When the size or combat role of the Guard is challenged, the Army normally supports the Guard. The Army Department has an interest in maintaining ground combat reserve forces. According to Army doctrine, such forces will have a role in future wars. Furthermore, Guard units constitute a substantial part of the Army organization. Their existence increases the amount of money and material under Army administration and provides slots for Regular Army officers as instructors. In 1958 Army Secretary Wilber M. Brucker and Chief of Staff Maxwell D. Taylor both urged Congress to maintain the Guard at 400,000 men.[33] Privately, Brucker was urging the NGA to lobby harder. In 1953–54 Army support within the Pentagon helped forestall proposals for relieving the Guard of its combat role. General Walsh at the time attributed success to the "united front" of the Army and the Guard. The willingness of Army leaders to defy administrative discipline in 1958 was undoubtedly encouraged by confidence in the chances of success—a confidence grounded in the NGA's reputation for influence. Similarly, the Army has sometimes resisted Defense Department pressure for actions adverse to the Guard on the grounds that the NGA's influence makes such action unfeasible. "We can't do that—the Guard won't stand for it," the Army objects. The NGA's record of success and its manifest capacity for organized protest make the Army's objection plausible.

Propaganda. Though it is a standard technique of pressure groups, propaganda—the conscious attempt to shape others' attitudes—has only recently been seriously undertaken by the National Guard Association. Until the middle 1940's, the NGA issued almost no obvious propaganda. After General Walsh became president, it issued a few pamphlets, but not until 1958 did the NGA hire a staff member with public relations skills.

The activity of the public information office in the National Guard Bureau had reduced the need for propaganda by the NGA. The purpose of the Bureau's program is to encourage recruiting, but it does not require a very broad interpretation of that purpose to justify advertising that creates a favorable "public image" for the Guard. TV and radio commercials have been used, with themes broad enough to impress the general public. The NGA's need for propaganda was reduced too by the circumstance that the Guard's interests rarely have implicated a large public. The issues in which the Guard is engaged ordinarily compel the attention of only a small group of congressmen, Defense Department officials, and (sometimes) Reserve leaders. But perhaps the most important explanation for the NGA's long-standing indifference to propaganda is that congressional attitudes have been so favorable to the Guard that propaganda seemed superfluous. Evidently this is no longer the case.

The six-months' training controversy spurred the NGA to hire a public relations man. Many newspapers criticized the NGA for objecting to the training requirement, and in a Gallup Poll, a heavy majority of respondents opposed the Association's position and a smaller majority favored federalization of the Guard. As the controversy drew to a close, General Walsh observed to Colonel James B. Deerin, then public information chief in the National Guard Bureau, that the Army Guard

was not now being sold at the grass roots, which accounted for the bad press of the past week, and that it was essential that such a campaign be started as soon as possible. It was also stressed that officers and non-commissioned officers at the unit level lacked the knowledge and did not have the time to do the job, and therefore it would have to be done at the Association level and on a strictly professional basis.[34]

When his active duty in the Bureau expired at the end of 1957, Deerin joined the NGA to undertake the highly ironic task of selling the Guard "at the grass roots." Since then the Guard has issued a number of brochures directed principally at Congress and speeches for use of local commanders. It has begun to sponsor essay contests for high school students, offering $2500 a year in cash prizes. The NGA's propaganda emphasizes three themes: states' rights, the symbolism of the citizen-soldier, and the military value of the Guard.

In addition to the obvious items of NGA propaganda—brochures and the like—certain other of the NGA's actions are designed to shape the attitudes of Congress or some broader public. For instance, the NGA has sometimes advanced policy proposals that it certainly did not want or expect to have adopted but were intended to put the Guard in a favorable light. In 1954, rather than oppose the President's National Reserve Plan outright, the NGA proposed as an alternative that men be drafted into the Guard. The NGA was not enthusiastic about this. The idea had precipitated a serious schism in the Association. It was proposed formally in order to spare the NGA from seeming to act in a negative role and to demonstrate the Guard's concern for national defense. Similarly, in 1958 the NGA began to emphasize the value of the Guard as a home defense force. The purpose was to encourage political support for the Guard from the governors and in Congress when the Defense Department first proposed to cut the Guard. If the Defense Department had seriously proposed revising the Guard's mission to give greater emphasis to home defense, the NGA would no doubt have objected strongly. Such tactics are a form of propaganda.

The effects of propaganda, even more than the NGA's other modes of influence, are hard to assess. They are probably negligible. The NGA's recent interest in propaganda may be of significance chiefly as evidence of adverse change in the Guard's traditionally favorable environment. That the NGA should feel a need to commission essays by high school students suggests that its influence, however much flaunted, may not be securely founded.

EFFICACY OF THE NGA: POSSIBILITIES

The successes of the NGA in the cold-war years are fairly clear, and they are undeniably impressive. In 1953–54, the NGA discouraged the authors of the New Look from proposing a home defense mission for the Guard. In 1957, when the Army sought to require six-months' active duty training of all Guard recruits, the NGA successfully invoked congressional intervention. As a result, the requirement was delayed for several months and the obligations of Guard service were reduced so as to provide fresh incentives to recruits. Guard strength jumped after the directive went into effect. Beginning in 1958, the NGA for several years got Congress to sustain the Army Guard's strength at 400,000 men in the face of repeated requests by the President for reduction. Congress appropriated funds for 400,000, and three times it enacted language requiring the Defense Department to spend the money. The Guard's basic goals have been satisfied. It has preserved a combat role and maintained a high level of strength.

What the Guard is able to achieve depends upon what Congress is willing and able to give it. Because the executive branch has become almost inaccessible, the NGA must make its approach through Congress even when the action it seeks to influence is an executive one. When the NGA faces an issue, its first step is always to invoke congressional authority, if possible. It tries to get Congress involved. This is a great deal easier to do in some cases than in others.

The optimum situation for the Guard is one in which the executive branch, in order to achieve its objectives, must ask Congress for legislation adverse to the Guard. This was potentially the case in 1953–54 when the Defense Department was contemplating conversion of the Guard into a home defense force. To achieve this, it would have been necessary to amend existing law. In such a case, the mere threat of NGA opposition before Congress is enough to inhibit the executive branch from making a proposal, for it knows that Congress will protect the Guard's interests. It is out of the question that Congress should pass legislation clearly detrimental to the Guard. The situation in 1953–54, if this analysis is correct, was analogous to that of 1944–45, described in Chapter III, when the War Department elected not to propose major changes in the Guard's mission or organization to Congress because it knew they would be rejected.

Another possibility, less favorable to the Guard, is a situation in which Congress has authority to veto action adverse to the Guard. The executive proposes a course of action that the Guard opposes, and the Congress may prevent this action by objecting or declining to concur. This has been the case in budget matters. The executive has proposed cuts in the Guard, and Congress has refused to agree. It has appropriated more money than the executive branch has asked for, and has enacted language requiring the executive to spend the money.

A third possibility, least favorable to the Guard, is a situation in which Congress has no formal authority. In such cases it is sometimes possible to invoke the informal intervention of Congress. This occurred in 1957, during the dispute over the Army's training directive. Congress need not have become involved in this controversy. Congressional action was not required to make the directive take effect. If the NGA had not demanded congressional action, none would have been taken. The NGA president announced when the directive was issued that "The Guard's strong opposition will be taken to Congress, where the matter will be settled." [35] The NGA then barraged Congress with appeals for help.

How Congress responds to the NGA's appeals for intervention and support depends heavily on the nature of the Guard's claims. Aside from the question of how much authority it has, Congress is more willing to respond in some cases than in others. The issue over Guard strength in 1958 and subsequent years illustrates the kind of claim to which Congress most readily responds.

In this case the Guard's interests were obviously at stake. A reduction of manpower is the most direct of threats. This meant that the Guard was united on the issue. Second, the Guard's claim was clearly defensive. The Guard was asking to retain what it had. Third, defending the Guard in this case did not damage the Reserves. Indeed, Congress defended the two simultaneously. The Defense Department tried to cut both, and Congress protected both. Fourth, the public costs of maintaining the Army Guard at 400,000 men were not great as such costs are reckoned in the Guard's sphere of interest, national defense. The cut of 40,000 men proposed by the Defense Department in 1958 would have saved only $38 million in Fiscal Year 1959. Most of this was for pay that presumably would be spent in the Guard members' home towns. Furthermore, it was possible to argue that it would contribute something to national defense. Maintaining the strength of the Guard could plausibly be defended on the grounds of public interest, at least to the satisfaction of most congressmen.* Finally, the NGA had the support of the Army Department. NGA staff members say that the Army's support was crucial to the Guard's success. It en-

---

* In 1962 Representative Robert L. F. Sikes, a member of the Defense Appropriations Subcommittee, told the House: "The cost of the reserves is a small fraction of our defense cost; yet the reserves are as vital to our national survival as any other element of our defense structure. All of us will be pleased that the committee has seen fit again to include sufficient funds to preserve the present strength of the Army Reserve and the Army National Guard. This requires a relatively small addition to the budget as submitted by the Pentagon. Yet this addition is vital to the maintenance of a sound defense posture and a modern, trained, equipped Reserve Force in the Army." (*Congressional Record*, 108:6849, April 17, 1962.)

hanced the merits of the Guard's case in congressional eyes and assuaged the normal congressional reluctance to alter presidential recommendations on force levels. In general, then, the NGA's chances for success are greatest when the Guard's interests are obviously at stake, the NGA is united in support of the claim, the claim threatens the interests of no other group, and there is support for the claim from a source in the Defense Department (presumably the Army).

Basically, Congress responds to the Guard for reasons that have been stressed throughout this book: the Guard's foundation in the Constitution, the state capitols, and home-town communities; its patriotic character; and its worthy purposes. These factors predispose Congress to help the Guard, and the NGA exploits this predisposition through use of the assets of influence just analyzed. There is, however, another important explanation for the willingness of Congress to respond to the Guard. Congress' action follows as well from its own interests in relation to the executive branch. When the NGA asks Congress to assert its authority at the expense of the Defense Department, Congress stands to gain as surely as does the National Guard.

The outcomes of the six-months' training controversy in 1957 and of the controversy over Guard strength in 1958 and subsequent years must be viewed in part as victories of Congress over the executive branch rather than as victories of the Guard over either. There is strong evidence that in neither case was Congress simply responding to the influence of the NGA. Instead Congress was exercising its own judgment and authority in an area of public policy—defense—that it considers important.

The guardian of congressional authority in both cases, as in most military matters during the cold-war years, was Representative Carl Vinson, of Georgia, veteran and very powerful chairman of the House Armed Services Committee. In the training controversy, he became a broker between the Army and the Guard, asserting his authority to impose a solution. After the controversy had gone on for a week or so, he summoned the NGA president to declare that it must be ended. At the same time, he called on the Army to reach a settlement. He then got both sides to sign a "memorandum of agreement." This memorandum reflected concern for the interests not only of the Guard and the Army, but also of Congress. Perhaps the most significant paragraph was one that committed the Army to maintaining Guard strength at the figure "determined in annual appropriations of the Congress." [36] This was the work of Vinson, not the NGA, and it had the effect of engaging his prestige and authority in the fight over Guard strength the next year.

Vinson and his Armed Services Committee were the Guard's earliest and staunchest supporters in the drive for maintaining the Army Guard's strength at 400,000. The committee held hearings on the proposed reduction and passed a resolution opposing it. Vinson personally urged the House Defense Appropriations Subcommittee to provide funds for a 400,000-man Guard. He need not have become involved in this issue at all. Action was up to the Appropriations Committee. But Vinson had a stake in the Guard's strength because of the 1957 memorandum and because there was a constitutional question at stake that involved the power of Congress over military policy. The question of Guard strength posed once more a recurrent problem of the cold war: whether Congress can force unwanted military expenditures on the executive branch. In general, the executive branch has refused to spend money for manpower or weapons beyond what it has sought in budget requests. Vinson has taken the position that this flouts the constitutional power of Congress. He appears to have seen a chance in 1958 to assert congressional authority on this issue by taking a firm stand on Guard strength.[37]

The chances of making congressional action effective were

better in the case of Guard strength than in most other disputed spending issues, including the strength of other ground components. One reason was that Congress was united in support of maintaining Guard strength. As Huntington has pointed out, Congress' ability to impose unwanted military expenditures on the executive branch is largely a function of the extent to which members of Congress—in particular, those on the Armed Services committees and Defense Appropriations subcommittees—agree among themselves on the action.[38] A second reason was that the executive branch implicitly acknowledges that Congress has a special interest in the reserve forces. In 1958 the Eisenhower Administration was seeking to cut the Regular Army, Marines, and Army Reserve as well as the Guard. Many congressmen believed that this policy was wrong, and some might have preferred to increase the regular forces instead of the Guard. In 1959 Vinson said that he would.[39] But it was easier for Congress to enforce its will with respect to the Guard. In 1958 the Senate Defense Appropriations Subcommittee, in response to a suggestion from the NGA, adopted language that required the Defense Department to spend funds for a 400,000-man Army Guard. On the Senate floor, minimum strengths were adopted also for the Army, Marines, and Army Reserve. Those for Army and Marine strength were dropped in conference. That for the Army Reserve was dropped the next year, although extra funds were provided and the Administration promised that they would be spent. Congress retained only the one for the Guard. "The logic behind our action in this case," explained the chairman of the House Defense Appropriations Subcommittee, "was that the National Guard is more of a State organization than is the Army Reserve."[40]

Congress feels that it has a broader right to legislate for reserve forces in general, and for the Guard in particular, than for other components of the military establishment. The executive branch in turn acknowledges this right. When Congress was threatening to enact minimum strengths for all of the ground components in 1958, the White House sought removal of them with the promise that reserve strengths would be maintained at the figures appropriated for by Congress, but it would make no such commitment with respect to the regulars.

The reserves "belong" to Congress because they are constituents, and the Guard "belongs" more than other reserve components because of its foundation in the states. Congress' possessiveness is nowhere better illustrated than in the statements of Mr. Vinson. In 1962 he told Congress:

Let me briefly say this. Who controls the reserve? The Congress of the United States controls the reserve. Who can say how many reservists can be called up except under a national emergency? The Congress of the United States. . . . I believe in the Congress meeting its responsibilities and I believe in keeping our custody and our control over the National Guard and the Reserves. So much for that, Mr. Chairman.[41]

In hearings in 1962, Vinson told the secretary of defense:

Mr. Secretary, if you go to breaking up the units in the Army National Guard, why we will have to have a talk up here. [Laughter]
We are backing the Army National Guard. We are not going to sit quietly by and permit these units to be broken up and for individuals to be plucked out of the units. . . .
You leave our National Guards alone.
Because, you see, Mr. Secretary, the National Guard is a State organization. . . .[42]

Congress' possessiveness toward the Guard is heightened by antagonism between the Guard and the Defense Department. Congress, according to Senator Saltonstall, feels that the Defense Department "sits on the Guard." "When there comes a division of the dollar," another senator said in debate in 1962, "naturally the Regulars are looking after their own programs. . . . The National Guard must beg for a little facility . . . that would cost, for example, only $100,000."[43] Congress believes that it must protect the Guard's interests if they are to be protected at all. Experience shows that they will not be protected by Congress' rival, the executive branch.

In taking a special interest in the Guard and reserve forces generally, Congress is performing its representative function. The executive branch acknowledges the necessity of this function and makes limited concessions to Congress' interest in reserve matters. This being so, Congress can use issues involving the Guard to demonstrate its authority over military affairs. Congress' interest in serving its constituents and its interest in asserting authority vis-à-vis the executive branch in military matters coincide in the case of some important issues involving the Guard.

EFFICACY OF THE NGA: LIMITS

To analyze the efficacy of the NGA, it is necessary to explain what it cannot do as well as what it can. The Guard's political achievements are plainer than its political limitations, but they are not on that account of greater importance in defining what it can get from government. In some matters, Congress is not willing or able to help the Guard. It may be inhibited by a lack of authority or by political obstacles, or it may disapprove the content of the Guard's claim.

Although Congress has challenged the Defense Department boldly over Guard strength, with respect to many Guard matters it defers to the executive more than it did before World War II. According to the NGA staff, the Guard cannot get legislation from Congress that the Army genuinely opposes. This was not always the case. Earlier in the century, Congress showed little hesitancy in exercising its own judgment on Guard affairs or following the advice of the NGA. With the growth of the Defense Department and the increased complexity and technicality of military problems, Congress has grown more cautious. It defers to the executive less on matters involving the Guard than on other aspects of defense policy, but it defers more on Guard matters than it once did. This point is well illustrated by a diary item of March 22, 1950, in which General Walsh recorded disappointment over the refusal of the House Appropriations Committee to grant the Guard all of a requested budget increase:

> Information received indicates Mahon [chairman of the Defense Appropriations Subcommittee] called General Collins [Army chief of staff] to find out if the Guard really needed [the money]. His action is in contrast to that of his predecessors, Albert Engel of Michigan and Ross Collins of Mississippi, who did their own thinking rather than being rubber stamps of the War Department.

That this is a fair characterization of Mahon is debatable (General Walsh tended to be critical of anyone who resisted the Guard), but it is probably sound evidence of increased congressional deference to executive opinions.

Congress is reluctant to presume authority with respect to organization of the Guard, for reserve organization theoretically derives from strategic planning, which Congress respects as the rightful province of the executive branch. Twice in recent years—in 1958 and 1962—the Defense Department sought to eliminate several Guard divisions as part of a comprehensive reorganization of the Guard. Congress both times took a passive view of this threat, at least by comparison with its view of a reduction in the Guard's numerical strength. To maintain the Guard at 400,000 men in 1958, Congress had assembled an array of weapons—resolutions by a House subcommittee and the House as a whole, appropriation of extra funds, and adoption of mandatory language in the appropriations act. With regard to unit strength, it did much less. The House subcommittee that took the initiative in defending the Guard's interests did not object explicitly to elimination of the divisions. Instead, it called on the Army to proceed with revising the Guard's troop basis "with the advice and assistance of the Army National Guard Committee [the Section Five Committee]," and stipulated that the new organization should be approved by the governors (which the law required in any case) and that the Armed Services committees should be informed of organizational changes. This was an elaborate expression of interest in Guard reorganization, but far from an admonition not to eliminate the divisions. The Guard did succeed that year in retaining the threatened divisions, apparently because the Army was less than determined to make the cuts. Governors and adjutants general vigorously protested the cuts to the secretary of defense and secretary of the army throughout the spring of 1958; in May, Army Chief of Staff Maxwell D. Taylor announced to the Governors' Conference that the divisions would be kept. The Army, in a struggle against the New Look doctrine, was trying to retain reserve ground forces if it could not retain active ones.

In 1962, however, the Guard failed to prevent a reduction of four divisions. Again, Congress reacted passively to the threat to the Guard. In a typical demonstration of concern for community interests, Congress did seek to assure that no town would lose a Guard unit. It wrote into the Defense Appropriations Act a provision that "insofar as practicable in any reorganization [of the Guard] . . . the geographical location of existing units will be maintained." This was not tantamount to opposing elimination of the divisions. A House Armed Services subcommittee, in the course of a harsh report on the Defense Department's handling of reserve policy, conceded that "It is not the subcommittee's intention to question a military decision which determines that eight Reserve and Guard divisions are no longer required in the Reserve Establishment." [44] The subcommittee chairman, F. Edward Hébert, wrote the secretary of the army that the subcommittee would have no objection to Guard reorganization as long as the governors approved. Congress in effect left the Guard to its own devices. The Guard's position this time was further weakened by lack of support from the Army, which was no longer threatened with a reduction of active strength. The Kennedy Administration had added two divisions to the Army, having decided that active forces should be strengthened at the expense of the reserves. Under these circumstances the Army could not be counted on for strong opposition to cuts in the Guard. The Guard itself was not as strongly united in opposition to the cuts as it needed to be. All four of the divisions proposed for elimination were ones that embraced more than one state: the 35th of Kansas and Missouri, the 34th of Nebraska and Iowa, the 43rd of Connecticut, Rhode Island, and Vermont, and the 51st of South Carolina and Florida. Not all of these states were hostile to the proposal. Some whose units had been subordinate to a division headquarters located in another state now stood to gain a brigade headquarters of their own, a prospect not displeasing to them.

The NGA's efforts to maintain the Army Guard's strength at 400,000 men also faltered in 1962. Congress again appropriated more funds for the Guard than the executive branch requested and enacted language requiring the Defense Department to program for a strength of 400,000—but Congress at the same time agreed to several conditions that made it unlikely that a strength of 400,000 would in fact be achieved. These conditions, as stipulated by the secretary of defense, were that Guard units apply the same recruiting standards as the active Army, not exceed authorized strength, and contain no more than one member in ten lacking an appropriate military occupational specialty.

There had always been considerable doubt whether Congress could or would indefinitely sustain the strength of the Army Guard at 400,000 men. The advantages in this issue lie with the President. He plans, proposes, and executes the budget, and in a military budget issue, he has the additional advantage of his authority as commander-in-chief. Despite Congress' success in enforcing a strength floor under the Guard, the weight of precedent continued to favor the President's position that he should be free, as commander-in-chief, to determine force levels. A substantial minority of congressmen on the Appropriations and Armed Services committees in 1958–1962 agreed with him even though Vinson did not. In 1962 the Defense Department found a formula to exploit the executive's institutional advantages. The recruiting conditions that it proposed were difficult for Congress or the Guard to take exception to without seeming to flout the public's interest in well-prepared reserve forces. As the Defense Department doubtless anticipated, these conditions depressed Guard strength, which dropped to 380,000 in 1963. The Department had succeeded in achieving indirectly what it failed to achieve directly through reduced appropriations for the Guard. In 1963, Congress for the first time in years appropriated funds for an Army Guard of less than 400,000 men, although it again enacted language requiring the Defense Department to program for a strength of 400,000. It invited a request for a supplemental appropriation if that strength were achieved. The Guard's position in defense of the 400,000-man figure, built up with so much effort by the NGA in 1958, was crumbling. Congress was retreating by stages from its earlier rigid stand.

Even when Congress clearly has authority to act in the Guard's favor, political obstacles sometimes stand in its way. One such obstacle arises from the practice of race discrimination in Guard organizations in the South. This is probably the principal remaining manifestation of state control over the Guard. The federal government cannot assign men who have a reserve service obligation to Guard units. (It can assign them to Reserve units.) For service in the Guard, they must "volunteer," although most do so as a way of fulfilling their obligation of military service to the federal government. This volunteer principle enables Guard organizations in the South to remain white. As of 1963, ten states had no Negro Guard members.

Segregation is a grave political liability for the Guard. It is a source of internal friction. In the early 1950's, when Guard leaders from New York State proposed solving a manpower shortage in the Guard by asking the federal government to draft men for Guard service, Southern Guard officers were violently opposed. General Reckord, from the border state of Maryland, threatened in 1953 to quit the NGA if it adopted the New Yorkers' proposal.[45] Segregation invites attempts by liberals to promote measures of federal control over the Guard. In 1963 Senator Jacob K. Javits of New York wrote the Defense Department asking what steps it was taking to achieve integration in the Guard. The Department replied that it was trying to get Guard organizations in the South to desegregate voluntarily. To cut off federal support from such units, it said, would not "at this time" be "in the national interest."[46] In addition, the practice of segregation potentially limits the capacity of Congress to act on behalf of the Guard. When the Reserve Forces Act came from the House Armed Services Committee in 1955, it provided for mandatory participation of Guard recruits in training for reserve service (what subsequently became the six-months' program). On the House floor, Negro Congressman Adam Clayton Powell attached antisegregation amendments to the bill. As a result, the provisions applying to the Guard were dropped. Although this action was not at the time unwelcome to the NGA, it proved to be a serious blow to the Guard's interests. What Congress failed to do by statute in 1955 the Army did by directive in 1957, in a major extension of executive authority over the Guard. Since 1955, all legislation affecting the Guard has run the risk of a new Powell amendment. As long as the Guard in Southern states remains segregated, the NGA's expectations of help from Congress have to be adjusted to this situation, and the increase of executive discretion in Guard matters is encouraged.

What Congress does for the Guard also depends very importantly on the nature of the Guard's claim. Though it is a staunch ally of the Guard, Congress is not an undiscriminating one. On several occasions during the cold-war years, the Guard has had to suppress or moderate a claim rather than risk defeat. On one occasion, in 1952, it had to accept defeat.

The Guard was never enthusiastic about the Armed Forces Reserve Act of 1952. When new reserve legislation was proposed in 1950–51, the NGA argued that changes should be accomplished by amendments to the National Defense Act and not by an entirely new act. The bill did not promise much for the Guard; it was intended primarily to benefit the Reserves. Nevertheless, the NGA had to acquiesce in preparation of the bill. As General Walsh later observed to the NGA Executive Council, "It was a case where all the other reserves were united with the powerful backing of the Administration." [47] When the bill passed the House in October 1951, the NGA endorsed it perfunctorily, but when it came before the Senate Armed Services Committee the following May, the NGA suddenly raised objections.[48]

The NGA's motives in opposing the act are not entirely clear. Apparently, the Association was not trying to defeat the act, but rather to have included in it a blanket draft exemption for Guard recruits. The NGA tried to exact this as the price of its support. Late in 1951 and early in 1952 the Guard's strength had dropped suddenly. This occurred partly because Congress, in the Universal Military Training and Service Act of 1951, had put an end to the Selective Service System's extralegal practice of deferring all enlistees in the Guard, even those who joined after the age of eighteen-and-a-half.* Because its strength was falling far short of its Fiscal Year 1952 program, the Guard received a

* The Guard has close, sympathetic ties with the Selective Service System. The state staffs of the Guard help administer Selective Service. A large majority of the state directors of Selective Service have been Guard officers, and many have been adjutants general, holding the two posts simultaneously. The veteran Director of Selective Service, Lieutenant General Lewis B. Hershey, is a frank partisan of the Guard (and of reserve forces in general). This has increased the Guard's influence on Capitol Hill, where General Hershey is much admired.

sharp reprimand from the House Appropriations Committee in the spring of 1952. The Committee cut $66,700,000 from the Guard's budget request. The NGA's opposition to the Armed Forces Reserve Act appears to have been a response to this situation rather than to the content of the act itself.[49] The opposition was futile. The Senate committee refused the NGA's demands.

This case is an illustration of the kind of issue on which Congress does not respond to the Guard. As such, it contrasts with the strength issue of 1958. In 1952 the Guard's stake was obscure. The NGA's leaders were not persuasive when they argued that the Armed Forces Reserve Act threatened the Guard. That the NGA had endorsed the bill in the House did not help their case any. Furthermore, not all Guard members supported the NGA's stand in 1952. After NGA officials had testified before the Senate committee, they got a number of calls from puzzled Guard officers who wondered what they were up to. The NGA's claim in 1952 was not clearly defensive. The request for a blanket draft exemption for Guard recruits may have seemed defensive from the Guard's perspective, inasmuch as it was meant to sustain a dwindling level of strength. From the perspective of Congress, however, it represented a demand for new legislation on behalf of the Guard. In 1952 the public costs of the Guard's claim promised to be high, and they could not plausibly be defended on the grounds that they served the public interest. It had already been made plain that if all Guard recruits were exempted from the draft, many men would join in the hope of avoiding active service in the Korean war. The NGA, in asking for a blanket draft exemption for Guard recruits, was pleading for something that Congress had specifically disapproved in 1951. The Guard's claim in 1952 threatened the Reserves. The ROA had been hailing the Armed Forces Reserve Act as the Reserves' "magna carta." When the NGA opposed the act, the ROA was furious. Finally, the NGA stood alone in 1952. Whereas in 1958 it had support from the Army Department, in 1952 it had no support from an executive source. Like the ROA, all Defense Department offices with an interest in the act were furious at the NGA's impromptu effort to kill or amend it. This case tends to confirm the earlier analysis, by suggesting that the Guard fails when its interests are not obviously at stake, its members are not united, its claim is not defensive, the public costs of granting the claim would be high, the claim threatens the interests of the Reserves, and there is no support for the claim from an executive source.

Further support for some of these points is available from other cases. In no other instance has the NGA suffered overt, unequivocal defeat, but that is only because it has learned to behave with circumspection. It does not make claims upon Congress unless the conditions for success can be met.

The NGA's restraint is well illustrated by its attitude toward the Reserve Forces Act of 1955. When this was before Congress, the NGA took a cautious, equivocal public position even though it privately regarded the act as detrimental to the Guard's interests. When the adjutant general of Iowa observed to General Walsh that the act ought to be killed, General Walsh "agreed with him but pointed out the full force of the Administration was behind H. R. 2967, and further, that it was a question as to what Congress would do."[50] It is no longer feasible for the Guard to oppose congressional actions that benefit the Reserves. Before World War II and for a brief time after, the NGA exercised a veto over such legislation, but its veto power is now much restricted. Indeed, growth of the reserve forces bureaucracy in the Defense Department, which has been seriously detrimental to the Guard, has occurred partly as a result of congressional interest in helping the Reserves. The Guard therefore can do nothing about it. To appeal to Congress for relief from Congress' own actions would be both embarrassing and futile. The freedom of the Guard to defend itself is peculiarly circumscribed also by the nature of the issues in which it is involved. If the Guard seeks to prevent development of the Reserves, it runs the risk of seeming unpatriotic.

Nor can the NGA exercise influence in matters not directly engaging the Guard's interests. Ordinarily, it does not try. When it did try once, in 1955, the effort proved futile. Army Chief of Staff Matthew B. Ridgway had appealed to the NGA for help in preventing a reduction in the Army. According to General Walsh's account, Ridgway emphasized that

something must be done and quickly, and that the only agency that was strongly organized, thoroughly disciplined, and had the strength, influence and potency to undertake the mission is the National Guard Association. . . . After considerable discussion of the problem it was agreed that the National Guard Association would secretly undertake the mission, and during the week of 29 May would initiate discussions and measures, and would report on progress.[51]

General Maxwell D. Taylor, Ridgway's successor, repeated this appeal two months later. Again General Walsh agreed to help the Army, on the condition that in return it should acknowledge the "organizational, strength, and training status of the National Guard." [52] But there is no evidence that the NGA was able to do anything for the Army—no progress report, no claims to success, and, on the face of the record, no success. Army strength continued to dwindle. This was a problem beyond the range of the NGA's influence. By contrast, when the Guard's own strength was threatened, the NGA responded with remarkable effectiveness.

The NGA has recognized the necessity of being united when it takes a claim to Congress. On the single occasion in recent years when there was a serious split within the NGA over proposed legislation, the contending factions agreed that, because they could not agree, the proposal should rest. This was the proposal that the Guard should seek authority to acquire manpower through the draft, which the NGA debated in 1952–53.

The proponents backed down in the realization that unity was essential if the proposal were to be put before Congress with a chance of success.[53] The NGA later advanced it as an alternative to the National Reserve Plan of 1954, but without seriously expecting it to be adopted.

When Congress does not respond to a claim from the Guard, the NGA can do very little. Pressure is not effective. Despite the NGA's vigorous efforts at the time of the six-months' training controversy, Congress viewed the Guard's claims with considerable indifference. According to General Walsh's contemporary account to the adjutants general, Congressman Vinson planned to sponsor a concurrent resolution that would have ended the controversy with a compromise highly favorable to the Guard, but he changed his mind "for the simple reason that he doubted he could obtain the necessary number of votes." [54] The NGA had ineptly taken a stand "against training"—against military readiness in a period of national danger—and many congressmen apparently were reluctant to align themselves with the Guard in this awkward position. The terms of Vinson's memorandum of understanding were not as favorable as the NGA had hoped for. Nevertheless, when Vinson offered them, General Reckord advised General Walsh "that if the chairman and committee were so minded, the NGA had no choice but to accept." [55] Clearly, Vinson was not yielding to "pressure."

Similarly, the NGA in the early 1960's could not get the chairman of the Senate Armed Services Committee, Richard B. Russell, to respond to it. Among other things, the NGA was trying to pass a bill providing federal compensation for injury or disability to men attending state officer candidate schools, which the Guard runs under federal supervision. Russell would not even hold hearings on the bill. The NGA had sent telegrams to him and tried every tactic it could think of, all to no avail. This was but one of several minor matters on which Russell had failed to respond to the NGA. According to an NGA staff member, the problem was not that Russell was hostile to the Guard, but he was skeptical of its demands and a little jaded after many years of service in the Senate. "He has thought for a long time," this source said, "that there's too damn much military legislation." Nothing the NGA can do will make him take action if he does not want to.

In order to sustain success, the NGA must tailor its claims to suit the predilections of Congress. This is fundamental to its whole strategy of influence. Adjustment of claims also serves the very important purpose of sustaining one of the Guard's principal political assets, its reputation for influence. If this reputation were not of great value to the Guard, there would be negligible harm in making claims that could not be realized.

FUTURE OF THE GUARD

Adverse changes in the environment of the Guard will probably continue. Emphasis on missile power and on active-duty personnel will almost certainly increase. The future holds, too, increased centralization of power in the Defense Department. The Department's influence in Guard matters will continue to grow at the expense of Congress, and within the Department the influence of the National Guard Bureau will continue to decline.

In the future the Guard will find it difficult to respond to adverse environmental changes by intensifying the activity of the NGA. The Association is as fully organized as it can be, with 100 percent of its potential membership enrolled and paying sizable dues. Besides, it is difficult to see what more the NGA could do than it has been doing, except possibly increase its propaganda, which would not have much effect. NGA officials and observers of the NGA alike agree that it is exploiting its political assets to the maximum. It has reached the limits of its efficacy.

The NGA may find it difficult even to sustain the intensive

activity and the organizational cohesion for which it is well known. The character of the Guard organization is changing under the impact of the cold war. The Guard has long prided itself on being a volunteer organization. Men joined as privates, attracted by the glamour of military life or the social satisfactions of Guard membership, and worked their way up through the ranks, deepening their attachment to the Guard along the way. Their intense loyalty to the Guard impelled them to vigorous, united political activity. Today the incentives of Guard membership have changed. Though some men undoubtedly join, as Guardsmen always have, out of a spontaneous attraction to a military organization, most choose the Guard as one way—in their particular cases the most advantageous way—of fulfilling an obligation to the federal government. They view Guard service as a source of material benefits.

This emphasis on material benefits may in the long run prove quite troublesome for the Guard and NGA. It has already become a source of internal friction. Guard members place strong, steady demands upon the NGA for legislation conferring personnel benefits. They are encouraged in this by the NGA's reputation for omnipotence before Congress. As a way of evoking the pride and loyalty of the members, NGA leaders have long told them how influential the Association is and how much they owe to it in the way of material benefits. An NGA leaflet for distribution to Guard officers tells "what the Association has done for you and for national defense"—a list of eighteen pieces of legislation beneficial to the Guard. Guard members apparently believe all this, and want more. Their demands often embarrass NGA headquarters, which does not like to press their claims upon Congress. Rather than exhaust the NGA's resources of influence for such purposes, NGA headquarters often tries to stall the claims by submitting them for study by Association committees. When delays of this kind are exhausted, Association headquarters introduces the bill but does not press for passage.

Situations of this kind have lately strained relations between Association headquarters and its followers, and within Association headquarters, between the president and the professional staff. The staff, on whom the burden of lobbying falls, takes a more conservative view of the Guard's political influence than do the president or other members of the Association. It is concerned to limit the Guard's claims, whereas others in the Association continue to believe in the Guard's political invincibility.

Division of material benefits sometimes causes friction among state Guard organizations. The NGA recently got legislation authorizing federal contributions to the pension funds of the Guard's civilian technicians, but these benefits were contingent upon certain state programs, with the result that they were distributed unequally among the states. The disadvantaged states complained to Congress, in a few cases without first consulting NGA headquarters.

Within the NGA itself, the desire for material benefits may prove disruptive. NGA Presidents Walsh and Harrison were remarkably devoted to the Guard, but there is no assurance that their successors will always be equally so. The NGA pays its president an annual salary of $25,000, and there are some within the organization who feel that this may attract men who are more interested in the money than in protecting the Guard's political interests.

As the environment of the Guard becomes less manageable, the inability of the Association to get what Guard members want is likely to become an increasingly serious problem. Material wants may have to go unsatisfied, and so may some other desires of Guard members. If the Guard should be substantially reduced in strength, morale would be seriously affected. If Guard organizations in the South are forced to accept Negroes, the Association will probably be embarrassed by pressures from Southern Guard organizations to resist integration.

It seems probable that the Guard faces a political decline, but if so, the process will be gradual and prolonged. An organization that has been successful so long will not collapse suddenly, if only because the traditional practices of Congress protect it. Compromise—the principle by which issues are settled—will spare the Guard the embarrassment of a sudden, demonstrable defeat.

CHAPTER VI ✦ POWER AND TIME:
THE GUARD'S EFFORTS TO ADAPT

One advantage of studying the Guard is that it has been active as a pressure group for many years—over three-quarters of a century. The case allows an ample perspective in time, and this perspective helps to show how much the Guard's political fortunes have depended upon the momentary situation in which the Guard has found itself. The political history of the Guard does not consist of cumulative conquests by an all-but-irresistible lobby. Instead, there have been laborious, long-frustrated lobbying efforts; successes that were fruits of circumstance, made less satisfying by compromise; and struggle to prevent gains from being swept away by strong currents of environmental change. In retrospect, the impression generally is one of power— of goals fulfilled; but for this fulfillment, the Guard owes as much to fortuitous circumstance as it can claim credit for on account of its own political activity.

The Guard's success at any given time has depended heavily on the mood of Congress in military matters, and this in turn has depended on circumstances external not just to the Guard or even to Congress, but to the nation. The Guard has never been able to achieve major goals except when a need for military legislation seemed plausible to Congress. The Guard has also depended heavily upon having allies at crucial points in its political history. The outstanding example is Secretary Root, who secured passage of the Militia Act in 1903 and thereby laid the foundation for all of the Guard's subsequent achievements. The Guard has likewise benefited importantly from the absence of effective opponents to its political claims.

The Guard's dependence on environmental circumstances is further illustrated by the change of its political fortunes as those circumstances have changed. Over the long run, there has been a profound change in the values prevailing in Congress with respect to military questions, a change that has worked variously to the advantage and disadvantage of the Guard. The secular trend within Congress has been toward increasing acceptance of both the need for military legislation and concentration of the nation's military force under federal control. At the outset of the Guard's political history, antimilitarist and states' rights values were held so strongly in Congress that any legislation for the purpose of enhancing federal military power was difficult to pass. Under the impact of successive wars these values began to change. At first they were modified sufficiently to permit major legislation on behalf of the Guard, which was a useful vehicle for compromise whenever Congress experienced the tension between demands for, on one hand, more federal military power, and, on the other, adherence to the states'-rights and antimilitarist traditions. The long-term change in congressional values was, then, at first favorable to the Guard, which was enabled to realize its claims for added federal support. But as the change progressed and, after the start of the cold war, accelerated, the Guard's advantage began to diminish. The Guard began to be subjected to a degree of federal control so great as to threaten its autonomous existence as a state force, and, more important, it began to lose ground to its political rivals, the professional services and the federal reserves. Although Congress has retained a special attachment to the Guard on account of its foundation in the states, the relative advantages that the Guard once enjoyed on account of its citizen character and dual, federal-state status have greatly diminished.

The long-run change in congressional values with respect to military affairs has been associated with two other environmental changes of detriment to the Guard. One of these is the growth of the Guard's rivals. (This development is no doubt associated with a change in congressional conceptions of self-interest as well as of value; the Reserves' growth as a constituent group partly accounts for the change of congressional attitudes toward them.) The increased size and stature of the professional services and of the Reserves make them a source of competing claims which increase resistance to the Guard's goals. The second change has been an increase in the complexity of the Guard's environment. As recently as the 1940's the Guard could achieve success through the coordinated action of a relatively simple system of political actors, but during the cold war the number of actors with a share of authority over the Guard's affairs has increased substantially, and the potential resistance to the Guard's goals has increased accordingly.

All of these changes in the Guard's environment have, over the long run, made its goals more difficult to achieve. The Guard has been faced, as any pressure group must be, with the problem of keeping the magnitude of its achievements in balance with the magnitude of its goals. Its responses to this problem fall into four categories: (1) attempts to influence its environment so as to preclude resistance to its goals; (2) attempts to build defenses against adverse environmental change; (3) attempts to increase its capacity to overcome resistance; and (4) modification of goals.

THE GUARD'S INFLUENCE ON ITS ENVIRONMENT

Though its political fortunes have depended heavily upon the circumstances of its environment, the Guard has not been entirely without influence over those circumstances. Much of the Guard's political activity has, in fact, consisted of efforts to shape the structure of the environment within which that activity is carried on. To make this point clearer, it may be helpful to use a distinction between substantive goals—those that the Guard values for its own sake—and instrumental goals—those that are means to substantive ends. Substantive goals would include legislation giving the Guard status as a reserve force to the

Army, authorization of appropriations for it, and the actual appropriations acts, all of which contribute directly to the Guard's maintenance. Most of the goals that may be termed instrumental involve efforts of the Guard to shape its environment so as to make substantive claims easier to realize. The most important of these efforts have been directed toward two ends: forestalling development of rivals, and promoting development of allies.

One of the major political goals of the Guard has long been to retard development of a federal reserve force that might compete with it. Occasionally, as in 1898, the Guard has objected to increases in professional forces, but this has been rare; the Guard has generally viewed a federal reserve, not the Regular Army, as its principal rival. Preventing growth of this rival is an instrumental goal; it does not contribute directly to maintenance of the Guard. But insofar as the Guard has succeeded in achieving this goal (and for a long time its success was complete, or nearly so), the effect has been to eliminate a major potential obstacle to the Guard's substantive successes. By discouraging development of a rival force, the Guard discouraged an important source of competing claims that would have made its substantive goals harder to realize. (The Guard's objections to a federal reserve force were not the sole cause of Congress' delay in creating one, but the Guard's resistance to the idea was a contributing factor in the delay, and to that extent, the Guard helped shape its environment.)

Another major goal of the Guard has long been to see that administration of its affairs on the federal level is performed by a friendly agency. For this purpose, the Guard promoted development of the National Guard Bureau as a semiautonomous administrative agency with wide authority in Guard matters. It also promoted development of the Section Five committees as agencies with jurisdiction over federal policies for the Guard. In both cases, the purpose of the Guard has been to shape its environment so as to make its substantive goals easier to realize.

It has sought to influence the composition of the system of political actors having authority over Guard affairs, with the aim of keeping the system simple and accessible and thereby minimizing resistance to its substantive claims. The Guard's efforts to retard development of rivals and promote development of allies have been manifested in claims on Congress. The federal reserve forces and the administrative agencies with authority over Guard affairs are to a considerable extent creatures of Congress, with an express foundation in legislation. That which receives statutory expression has been relatively open to the Guard's influence, given the receptivity of Congress to the Guard's claims. However, some elements of the institutional setting within which the Guard works are fixed not by statute, but by the Constitution. That which has received constitutional expression is much harder to influence, yet even such of the structure of its environment as is constitutionally determined is not entirely beyond the Guard's influence. The role of Congress in the formation of military policy is prescribed in the Constitution; so is the role of the President. Hence the relations between executive and legislative branches in military matters derive fundamentally from constitutional clauses, but years of interpretation and usage have added unwritten meaning to them—and the Guard (as any pressure group) may help to shape interpretation and usage. Any pressure group has at least a small range of choice in determining the targets of its claims, or if not the targets, the occasions on which claims will be directed toward those targets. If Congress has exercised a large amount of authority in Guard matters, this is only partly because the Constitution says it shall, and only partly because Congress is interested in the Guard as a constituent group. The Guard itself is to some extent responsible, because it has repeatedly and insistently addressed claims to Congress. The result has been to help induce Congress to take a large and active role in Guard matters, and this in turn facilitates realization of the

Guard's claims. Contributing to constitutional custom and usage thus is one way the Guard has influenced its environment.

Perhaps the way in which a pressure group is most commonly thought to shape its environment is through influence on the processes, either electoral or appointive, by which individual incumbents are chosen to fill particular roles of authority bearing on the group's claims. Pressure groups are thought to exercise their influence by contributing to the selection for office of persons who favor them or to the removal of persons who are hostile. The Guard has engaged in some activity of this kind, as when the NGA takes an interest in who the National Guard Bureau chief will be or how it can secure appointment of a friendly civilian to an executive post in the Defense Department. However, this kind of activity represents a small fraction of the NGA's total effort, and the effects of it have been insignificant. Influencing the selection of individual office-holders, either in Congress or the executive branch, is for the Guard at most a peripheral mode of shaping its environment.

The Guard has enjoyed considerable success in influencing its environment, notably in retarding development of the Reserves and promoting development of the National Guard Bureau, but its success even in these respects has not been enduring. Eventually the pressures for creation of a large federal reserve force became too great for the Guard to resist. Nor has the Guard been able to prevent growth of a complex reserve affairs bureaucracy that has undermined the long-standing hegemony of the National Guard Bureau. The Guard's environment is too complex for it to control. The influence that the Guard has been able to exert on its environment has been sporadic rather than sustained, and marginal in its effects.

DEFENSE AGAINST ENVIRONMENTAL CHANGE

The Guard has constructed strong defenses against adverse environmental change. Sometimes it has done so purposefully—

as when General Reckord, in 1940, got Congress to include the "National Guard protective clause" in the Selective Service Act. More often, the Guard's defenses have been constructed as an incidental (but important) byproduct of favorable legislation in general.

If Congress set out today to design the defense forces of the United States anew, it might not include the National Guard as the principal reserve force. But more than sixty years of statutes cannot easily be erased, especially when 47,000 members of the National Guard Association are prepared to object that their interests would be injured. That the members of the Guard are recruited under federal statutes, paid with federal money, equipped with material procured by the federal government, and drill in armories largely paid for with federal funds makes the Guard no easier to disestablish. On the contrary, the benefits received from government help establish the Guard as a substantial group with a legitimate claim upon the government.

Broadly speaking, actions by government on behalf of the Guard have contributed to its defense in two ways: there has been an accretion of statutory precedents and administrative practices that serve as a barrier to actions adverse to the Guard; and the strength and stature of the Guard organization, and hence its capacity to defend itself, have grown. With the support of the federal government, the Guard has evolved from a collection of scattered, voluntary units into a highly organized, well-equipped force of more than 400,000 men. Such a group is capable of putting up strong resistance to adverse change. It can plausibly claim that it deserves protection as an established, long-sanctioned interest. Each favorable action on behalf of the Guard incidentally contributes something to its barriers of defense against its environment.

The Guard has built some defensive barriers deliberately. This purpose has been manifested in efforts to have federal policies with respect to the Guard put in statutory form, so that a minimum is left to administrative discretion. Once statutory commitments have been obtained, the burden of altering the *status quo* is placed on the Guard's opponents and made as heavy as possible. The Guard, in its own defense, needs only to prevent existing statutes from being altered—an easy thing to do. During debate over the continental army in 1916, during World War II, during the dispute over the Gray Board report after World War II, and during the New Look controversy of 1953–54, the principal strength of the Guard lay in the circumstance that it could rest its case on old laws, while its opponents had to seek new ones.

How useful such defenses are depends on the strength of the attack upon them as well as the extent to which the statutory formulations have a foundation in actual practice. Statutory provisions may be of little use for defense if they lack concrete content. An example is the Guard's protective clause, which provides that the Guard, "an integral part of the first line defenses of the United States," will be called up ahead of other reserves in an emergency. When the Korean war broke out, this was promptly suspended to permit immediate call-up of federal reservists. The clause provides as well that the strength and organization of the Guard will be "maintained and assured at all times," but inasmuch as it does not say how much strength will be maintained, which is the crucial question, its practical effect is negligible. The NGA fights to protect the clause whenever there is a possibility that it will be altered or eliminated, not because the language has practical significance, but because removal of the language from the statute books would be a symbolic defeat of great severity.

OVERCOMING RESISTANCE

The NGA is the Guard's vehicle for overcoming resistance to its claims, and one way that the Guard has sought to sustain its power has been by increasing the sophistication of the NGA and intensifying its activity. This has perhaps been the principal response of the Guard to the problems created in recent years by adverse changes in its environment. Such a response was open to the Guard because it had an unexploited potential for political organization.

The NGA, throughout its history, has been effective in two ways: it has communicated offensive claims (that is, for new action on behalf of the Guard) to those political actors having authority to grant them, and thus has stimulated them to activity (although the NGA's activity alone has rarely been a sufficient stimulus); and it has countered the claims of others (the War Department, the Defense Department, and the Reserves) with defensive claims in order to prevent detrimental action, and thus has neutralized the effect of others' resistance to its claims by putting up equal or greater resistance.

Fundamentally, then, the function of the NGA has been to formulate and communicate claims. In the case of offensive claims, its activity has helped to overcome the inertia of the system of actors to which they have been directed (as in 1903, when the NGA's long effort culminated, with the indispensable cooperation of Secretary Root, in the Militia Act). In the case of defensive claims, the NGA's activity or potential activity has sometimes stopped action altogether (as in the mid-1940's, when the mere threat of NGA opposition before Congress discouraged the War Department from an attempt to eliminate the Guard), and at other times, when action was impending, it has served to block off alternatives so that the course of action taken would be favorable to the Guard (as in 1916, when the NGA's opposition to the continental army helped foreclose that alternative and leave greater federal support for the Guard as the only possible course). Whatever the nature of the Guard's claims, they have not been advanced successfully except when environmental circumstances were propitious. The NGA's role—even during the peak years of its effectiveness, the late 1940's—has not been to shape congressional attitudes, but to take advantage, with timely, shrewdly aimed, and often repetitious claims, of favorable situations and a set of congressional attitudes generally favorable to the Guard irrespective of the NGA's activity. The resistance the NGA has overcome has been the resistance associated with congressional inertia or with ineffectual political opposition (as from the War Department in 1916), and even then the NGA has been assisted by fortuitous alliances or events. Other types of resistance, arising from congressional skepticism (for example, with respect to a militia act in the late nineteenth century) or from more able and determined opposition (that of the War Department to a militia pay bill in 1910–1915) the NGA has not been able to overcome.

The increased activity of the NGA in recent years has not altered the Association's basic function; at most, the effect is to compensate for increases in the difficulty of carrying out that function. The function of formulating and communicating claims has become more exacting as a result of changes in the Guard's environment. One such change is the increase in the stature of its political rivals. The NGA has had to increase its potential for activity if only to be prepared to counteract the Reserves and the Defense Department before Congress. But other changes are equally important: there is more political business for the Guard to transact than ever before, the number of political actors with whom it must be transacted is greater than ever (as a result of the growth and increased complexity of the Defense bureaucracy), and getting their attention is harder than ever (both in Congress and the executive branch, the persons with most authority in Guard affairs are occupied with a wide range of military matters which make heavy demands upon their time). All of this means that the NGA must be a sophisticated and intensely active organization if it is to gather sufficient information to formulate claims and direct them to the appropriate political actors at the appropriate time. It is this kind of activity—and not the shaping of congressional attitudes—in which the modern NGA is engaged. It exists to communicate claims, not to convert congressmen to its point of view. Conversion is rarely required, and when it is the NGA lacks the resources to effect it.

There are limits to the efficacy of the NGA—limits that for the most part are determined externally, by the amount and kind of resistance that the NGA encounters. But there are also internal limits on its activity—limits determined by the amount of organizational resources that the members are willing to contribute. In the cold-war years the NGA has reached these limits, or very nearly so, after having enrolled all Guard officers and elicited sizable dues from them, as well as a high level of activity.

MODIFICATION OF GOALS

A fourth method of keeping goals and achievements in balance is modification of goals. Throughout its history, the NGA has, with varying degrees of conscious purpose, modified the content of the Guard's claims so as to reduce the amount of resistance they would encounter. This was done in the late nineteenth century, when the claim for a militia act was withdrawn temporarily in favor of the more modest claim for additional appropriations; in the opening decades of the twentieth century, when the NGA steadily moderated the Guard's claim to freedom from federal control in order to acquire more federal benefits; and in the 1950's, when the NGA began to withdraw the Guard's claims in opposition to the Reserves.

The Guard's capacity to adapt its goals to environmental circumstances was greater at the outset of the Guard's political life than it is today. This is the case for several reasons, of which the principal one is that the Guard at first lacked a sharply defined conception of its interests. There was a low level of consensus within the organization, and the effect was to widen the political alternatives available to it. At the outset, the Guard was a heterogeneous organization whose members were drawn to it for a variety of reasons. Some were socialites who liked the pomp and prestige associated with the Guard. Some were businessmen who saw it as a way of restraining the power of labor. Some were office workers who liked the exercise and fraternal association of the nights at the armory. Some were seriously interested in fighting wars. To most of the Guard's leaders it seemed that additional support and recognition from the federal government were desirable, but there was a wide range of difference over how desirable they were and what should be the conditions of their acquisition. To the extent that the Guard had common goals, they were general and vague in the extreme—and hence adaptable to the environmental situation of the moment. The political "victories" of the Guard in 1903 and 1916 may be called that because to do so accords with the view that happened to prevail in the Guard at the time, but there were dissenters in each case, and those who prevailed seem to have been bound more by vague common sentiment and by a disposition to accept uncritically what was politically possible than by a carefully articulated consensus of interest. The Guard found adaptation of goals relatively easy at this stage also because of the kinds of adaptation that were open to it then. Adaptations took basically two forms:

(1) The Guard could forgo future benefits, as when the NGA withdrew its claim to a militia act in the late nineteenth century. This was not a case of giving up something that the Guard already had, which would have been difficult to do, but merely of moderating aspirations for the time being.

(2) The Guard could subordinate one claim to another in a rank of preferences, as when in both 1903 and 1916 it sacrificed freedom from federal control, a major goal, in order to acquire federal legal status and material perquisites, another major goal. The Guard sacrificed its freedom by degrees, and the fact that it always retained some freedom obscured the significance

of its sacrifice. The Guard's freedom from federal control is, after all, relative. Any situation short of complete subjection to the federal government—that is, any situation short of abandonment of the militia clause and hence destruction of the Guard as a dual-status force—may be interpreted as one of "freedom" from federal control. Between the point of nearly complete freedom, which was the Guard's situation in the late nineteenth century, and nearly complete subjection, which is the situation today, was a wide range of alternatives which opened to the Guard the choice of successively sacrificing the goal of freedom from federal control to that of greater federal support until the point of nearly complete subjection was reached. The flexibility (or substitutability) of its claims helped make the Guard adaptable at the outset of its political history.

As time passed, the Guard's capacity to adapt its goals diminished. A basic reason was that these goals became more sharply defined as the Guard acquired federal support and began to evolve as a combat reserve. A process of selection of members began that eventually fixed the Guard's determination to function as the front-line reserve force to the Army. Men who did not share the organization's evolving purpose were discouraged from membership; those who did share it were attracted to the Guard. Moreover, the benefits acquired from the federal government— material, pay, professional advice, and so forth—became a shared interest to which Guard members developed a strong attachment. In their common possession of the perquisites of Guard membership—perquisites of which government was the source— Guardsmen found the grounds of consensus. They were drawn together to preserve the gains of the early years and protect the existence of the organization with which those gains were associated.

As the Guard acquired more benefits from government, its dependence on government increased. Increasingly, the resources with which the Guard was maintained came from government. This rendered the Guard vulnerable to environmental changes; if these resources should be withdrawn, the Guard's interests would be seriously damaged. The problem the Guard now faced was not to forgo future benefits, but to retain present ones that had become essential to its maintenance. An additional difficulty was that the Guard had "used up" much of the substitutability of goals that permitted a flexible response to environmental circumstances at the outset of its political history. The Guard's ability to trade freedom from federal control for federal benefits decreased as its margin of freedom diminished. Thus, the kinds of adaptation open to the Guard narrowed and became more difficult as time passed.

But if the Guard's capacity to adapt its goals diminished with time, so did the need to adapt them. The Guard's goals had become predominantly defensive. The drive to acquire benefits lost momentum and was superseded by a desire to protect what had already been acquired. Defensive goals ordinarily do not meet much resistance, at least by comparison to offensive goals. Because they involve preventing action by government rather than stimulating it, they are easy to realize unless opposed by very powerful counterclaims. For many years—throughout the interwar period and for several years after World War II—the Guard faced no such claims. And meanwhile it was developing a lobby that would strengthen its capacity to resist such claims should they come. The decrease in the Guard's capacity to adapt its goals tended to be offset, over time, by an increase in its capacity for political activity. The early lack of consensus with respect to goals had inhibited development of an effective lobby. When the Guard's conception of its interests had become firmly enough fixed to make adaptation of its goals difficult, it was firmly enough fixed to make lobbying easy. The "new" cohesive and active NGA was the result.

In recent years, even the defensive goals of the Guard have begun to encounter strong resistance. The Guard's claim to maintenance of its strength has been countered by the Defense Department's claim that Guard strength should be reduced. The Guard's claim to independence from federal control has been challenged several times, most importantly by the Army's training directive in 1957. Its claim to primacy as a reserve force has been challenged by the Reserves. Although the Guard's principal response to these events has been to intensify its own activity through the NGA, it has also responded by modifying its goals. In particular, it has withdrawn claims that conflict with those of the Reserves.

Modification of goals, like other modes of adaptation, can be undertaken only within limits. In this case, the limits are ones internal to the group, imposed by the group's own needs. The Guard, being heavily dependent on government for the resources of its maintenance, cannot sacrifice claims indefinitely without sacrificing itself out of existence. Thus far, its principal sacrifice has been of an instrumental goal—to restrain development of the Reserves—but substantive, and hence more costly, sacrifices may have to follow if resistance to the Guard's claims increases.

DECLINE OF THE GUARD'S POWER

The Guard's goals have fluctuated in magnitude. Its major offensive claims—for a militia act and then for armory drill pay—encountered insuperable resistance when first advanced, but this resistance subsequently disappeared under the impact of war. The Guard thereafter sought merely to maintain its situation, and in this it encountered little resistance until the cold-war years. Since the 1950's resistance to the Guard's defensive goals has risen, and with it, by definition, the magnitude of those goals.

The Guard's achievements have in general been commensurate with its goals, and thus its power has been sustained. Today, however, the long-established, more or less stable equilibrium between the Guard's goals and its achievements is threatened. As resistance to the Guard's goals increases, the magnitude of even its defensive goals is slowly exceeding the magnitude of its achievements. The Guard's power, which has been sustained for a long time, is beginning to decline. Its loss of four divisions in 1962 is important evidence of this.

The Guard has made various efforts to sustain its power. It has altered the content of its claims so as to encounter less resistance—but further alterations will be costly and difficult. It has intensified its political activity in an effort to maintain its capacity for achievement—but further intensification is infeasible and probably would be ineffective. Assuming a continuation of unfavorable trends in its environment and of the rise in resistance to its goals, the only possible outcome is a decline in the Guard's power.

The Guard's experience continues to suggest the great extent of its dependence on environmental circumstances. It carries on political activity in an environment that is infinitely changeable and imperfectly controllable. Although the Guard may adapt to external circumstances, its capacity to do so is limited rather than infinite. It is not inevitable on that account that the Guard should cease to be powerful. Environmental change can be favorable as well as unfavorable, and is not often completely one or the other. But to be so much at the mercy of it puts the Guard in peril.

NOTES

Chapter I. Group Power: The Case of the National Guard

1. The basic work on the role of pressure groups in the American system is David B. Truman, *The Governmental Process* (New York, 1951), which synthesizes a large literature. Since Truman's book the literature has grown much larger still, mostly with entries in a methodological debate over the utility of the concept of the group as an analytical tool. There is almost no scholarly literature on the National Guard. The only book is William H. Riker's brief case study in federalism, *Soldiers of the States* (Washington, 1957). Samuel P. Huntington analyzes the political influence of the Guard incisively in his theoretical work on civil-military relations, *The Soldier and the State* (Cambridge, Mass., 1957), pp. 169–177. Bennett M. Rich and Philip H. Burch, Jr., have discussed the Guard's development as a state agency of rescue and relief: "The Changing Role of the National Guard," *American Political Science Review*, 50:702–706 (September 1956). Other articles on the Guard include Frederick B. Wiener, "The Militia Clause of the Constitution," *Harvard Law Review*, 54:181–220 (December 1940), and Frederick P. Todd, "Our National Guard: An Introduction to Its History," *Military Affairs*, 5:73–86, 152–170 (Summer, Fall 1941). Some of the author's findings have been published in "Militia Lobby in the Missile Age: The Politics of the National Guard," in Samuel P. Huntington, ed., *Changing Patterns of Military Politics* (New York, 1962).

2. For data on the adjutants general, see Wisconsin, Legislative Reference Library, "The Adjutant General and the National Guard," Research Bulletin No. 112 (mimeo, Madison, 1953). For general information on state administration of the Guard, see James B. Deerin, *Guide for Army National Guardsmen* (Harrisburg, 1959), pp. 32–45.

3. *United States Code*, 1958 ed., Title 32, Ch. 1, Sec. 102.

4. On this point and more generally on the attachment of Guardsmen to their organization, see "You Get Imbued," by E. J. Kahn, Jr., *New Yorker*, 37:34–52 (January 13, 1962).

5. Interview, Major General Ellard A. Walsh, January 7, 1960.

6. Robert A. Dahl, "The Concept of Power," *Behavioral Science*, 2:201–215 (July 1957). Among other significant efforts are Harold D. Lasswell and Abraham Kaplan, *Power and Society* (New Haven, 1950); Herbert Simon, "Notes on the Observation and Measurement of Political Power," *Journal of Politics*, 15:500–516 (November 1953);

James G. March, "An Introduction to the Theory and Measurement of Influence," *American Political Science Review*, 59:431–451 (June 1955); and March, "The Power of Power," an unpublished paper delivered before the American Political Science Association in 1963 in which the author questions the utility of the concept "power" (shortly to appear in Leonard Binder and David Easton, eds., *Essays in General and Comparative Theory* [New York, 1964]).

7. Dahl, "Concept of Power," p. 209.

Chapter II. Years of Offense: 1879–1916

1. Francis V. Greene, "The New National Guard," *Century*, 21:483–498 (February 1892); War Department, Adjutant General's Office, Military Information Division, *The Organized Militia of the United States in 1896* (Washington, 1897), p. 5; H. R. Brinkerhoff, "The Regular Army and the National Guard," *United Service*, new series, 13:501–507 (June 1895).

2. Riker, *Soldiers of the States*, pp. 47 ff. For a typical contemporary comment, see *United Service*, first series, 2:394 (March 1880).

3. Major General George B. McClellan, "The Militia and the Army," *Harper's New Monthly Magazine*, 72:299 (January 1886); see also Colonel H. M. Boies, "Our National Guard," *Harper's New Monthly Magazine*, 60:915–923 (May 1880).

4. NGA Convention *Proceedings*, 1881, pp. 13–14.

5. Quoted in *The Citizen Soldier*, Boston, November 15, 1876, p. 1.

6. Walter Millis, *Arms and Men* (New York, 1956), p. 142.

7. *Journal of the Military Service Institution* (hereafter, *JMSI*), 2:413 (1881–82).

8. War Department, *The Organized Militia of the United States in 1896*, p. 164.

9. *Springfield Republican*, May 27, 1887.

10. The name "National Guard," derived from the French *Garde Nationale*, was first used by the Seventh Regiment of New York in honor of Lafayette when he was a visitor to this country in 1824. In 1862 the New York legislature gave the name to the entire militia force of the state. It was adopted in almost all of the states before 1900. Greene, "The New National Guard," p. 486n.

11. Arthur M. Schlesinger, *The Rise of the City, 1878–1898* (New York, 1933), p. 410.

12. *The Volunteers of America*, Proceedings of the Convention of National Guards, St. Louis, October 1, 1879, pp. 2–3.

13. NGA Convention *Proceedings*, 1897, p. 22.

14. *Congressional Record*, 18:295 (December 20, 1886).

15. *Congressional Record,* 24:446 (January 9, 1893).

16. *Reports* of the Secretary of War, 1878–1898 (for example, see the *Report* for 1880, vol. I, pp. vii–viii); James D. Richardson, *A Compilation of the Messages and Papers of the Presidents, 1789–1897* (Washington, 1900), IX, 115, 727. For a much fuller discussion of Army-Guard relations in this period, see Martha Derthick, "Citizen Soldier on Capitol Hill: the Political Life of the National Guard," unpub. diss., Radcliffe College, 1961, pp. 35–44.

17. *Congressional Record,* 26:8347 (August 9, 1894).

18. January 1, 1887. The *Journal,* which was the unofficial organ of the military profession, supported militia reform. See Donald N. Bigelow, *William Conant Church and the Army and Navy Journal* (New York, 1952), pp. 179–184.

19. For background on the war's impact on American society, see Walter Millis, *The Martial Spirit* (Boston, 1931), and Ernest R. May, *Imperial Democracy* (New York, 1961), chs. 11, 12. For the impact of the war specifically on the militia reform movement, see Colonel James G. Gilchrist, "The Reorganization of Our State Troops," *JMSI,* 23:418–426 (November 1898); Captain H. F. Davis, "Did the National Guard Fail in 1898?", *JMSI,* 24:417–421 (May 1899); Brigadier General Thomas M. Anderson, "In Re National Guard Essays," *JMSI,* 27:53–55 (July 1900).

20. General George W. Wingate, Comment on "The Reorganization of Our State Troops," *JMSI,* 23:552–555 (November 1898); Colonel James M. Rice, "The Recent Congress and the National Guard," *JMSI,* 19:452–479 (November 1896), which sets forth the views of this faction of the Guard; *Congressional Record,* 31:3626–3638 (April 6, 1898).

21. On the schism generally, see *Annual Reports of the Secretary of War, 1899–1903* (report for 1902), p. 289; for the viewpoint of the New York faction, Captain Herbert Barry, "In What Way Can the National Guard Be Modified So As to Make It an Effective Reserve to the Regular Army in Both War and Peace," *JMSI,* 26:207 (March 1960), F. R. Coudert, Jr., "The Proposed Reorganization of the National Guard," *JMSI,* 24:239–245 (March 1900), John F. O'Ryan, Comment on National Correspondence School for the National Guard," *JMSI,* 31:601–604 (July 1902), Charles S. Clark, "The Future of the National Guard," *North American Review,* 170:730–744 (May 1900).

22. Root to Redfield Proctor, December 12, 1902, Root MSS, Library of Congress; Major John H. Parker, "The 'National Guard' Problem," *Forum,* 28:190–196 (October 1899). For a recent argument that Root was no friend of the Guard, see Elbridge Colby, "Elihu

Root and the National Guard," *Military Affairs,* 23:23–24, 20 (Spring 1959).

23. Root to J. R. Hawley, January 24, 1902; Root to Henry Watterson and others, January 27, 1902; Root to J. M. Rice, December 12, 1902; Root to Redfield Proctor, January 7, 1903; Root to Richard W. Parker, January 14, 1903; all in Root MSS. See also Philip C. Jessup, *Elihu Root* (New York, 1938), I, 265–268, and *The "Dick" Bill and Comments . . .,* Publication No. 4 of the Interstate National Guard Association (February 1902).

24. *Congressional Record,* 35: 7708 (June 30, 1902) and 36:354–355, 395–398, 778–782 (December 16, 17, 1902, January 14, 1903); *Report of the Executive Committee of the Interstate National Guard Association,* Publication No. 5 of the INGA (July 1902), p. 16; Root to Redfield Proctor, January 20, 1903, Root MSS; Brigadier General William H. Carter, "The Organized Militia—Its Past and Future," *United Service,* third series, 3:789–794 (February 1903). Some years later Carter claimed that Root strongly opposed militia reform legislation unless it included authorization for the federal reserve, but this contradicts his own contemporary account. "The Militia Not a National Force," *North American Review,* 196:130–131 (July 1912).

25. Dick's papers are in possession of the Ohio Archaeological and Historical Society in Columbus. They include a brief biography, "Senator Charles Dick," a master's thesis submitted by Sister Mary Loretta Petit to the Catholic University of North America in 1948.

26. *U.S. Statutes-at-Large,* 32:775–780.

27. U.S. Congress, House of Representatives, *Hearings before the Committee on Militia . . . on H. R. 14783,* 1908; NGA Convention *Proceedings,* 1908, pp. 14–16; H. Rept. 1067, 60 Cong., 1 Sess. (1908); S. Rept. 630, 60 Cong., 1 Sess. (1908); *U.S. Statutes-at-Large,* 35:399.

28. *Congressional Record,* 42:6939–6946 (May 25, 1908); NGA Convention *Proceedings,* 1909, pp. 81–82.

29. *JMSI,* 42:312–314 (March–April 1908); *Report of the Secretary of War,* 1909, p. 59; Lieutenant Colonel A. W. A. Pollock, "The 'National Guard': A Hint from the United States," *Nineteenth Century,* 46:910–920 (November 1909); Captain Rutherford Bingham, "A Brief Study of Some of the Conditions Responsible for the Inefficiency of the Organized Militia and Their Cure," *JMSI,* 45:358–367 (May–June 1911); NGA Convention *Proceedings,* 1910, pp. 20–21; H. Rept. 2165, 61 Cong., 3 Sess. (1911).

30. For more on the activities of this group, see S. Doc. 621, 62 Cong., 2 Sess. (1912); *War Department Annual Reports,* 1912–1915; Henry L. Stimson and McGeorge Bundy, *On Active Service in Peace*

and War (New York, 1947), pp. 31–41; Hermann Hagedorn, *Leonard Wood: A Biography* (New York, 1931), II, 95–145; Millis, *Arms and Men*, pp. 193–203; Elting E. Morison, *Turmoil and Tradition* (Boston, 1960), pp. 144–177. For more on its conflict with the Guard, see Derthick, "Citizen Soldier on Capitol Hill," pp. 79–100.

31. NGA Convention *Proceedings*, 1914, p. 50.

32. A Guardsman wrote in 1912, "The greatest weakness of the [militia] system is the general officers. There are a few notable exceptions, but take them as a whole they would render inefficient, through no fault of their own save inexperience, the best trained troops in the world." Walter M. Pratt, *Tin Soldiers: The Organized Militia and What It Really Is* (Boston, 1912), p. 49. Despite its somewhat ambiguous title, this book is a defense of the Guard.

33. *Congressional Record*, 46:3223–3227 (February 23, 1911).

34. File 011.6, "Revision of the Militia Laws (Pay Bill)," and File 080, "National Guard Assn. of the U.S., Meeting, 1914," both in Record Group 168, National Archives.

35. The minutely detailed reports of the NGA executive committee chairmen for 1908–1914, which were published in the convention proceedings, read like manuals on how to lobby. The best summary of the NGA's techniques is in the *Proceedings* for 1911, pp. 17–27, 123–140.

36. The quotations are from a memoir by Hay (hereafter, Hay memoir), written some time between his retirement from Congress in 1916 and his death in 1931. It is one of a very few Hay manuscripts in the Library of Congress. On Hay's power, see also Hugh L. Scott to E. St. J. Greble, December 8, 1915, Scott MSS, Library of Congress; Garrison to President Wilson, January 12, 1916, *New York Times*, February 12, 1961, p. 2.

37. On the conflict between Ainsworth and the War Department, and, more specifically, on Hay's alliance with Ainsworth in the dispute, see Otto L. Nelson, Jr., *National Security and the General Staff* (Washington, 1946), pp. 109–166; Stimson and Bundy, *On Active Service*, pp. 33–37; Siert F. Riepma, "Portrait of an Adjutant General: The Career of Major-General Fred C. Ainsworth," *Journal of the American Military History Foundation*, 2:26–35 (Spring 1938).

38. Hay memoir.

39. W. F. Sadler, Jr., to J. P. Tumulty, October 23, 1915, and Wilson to Sadler, October 26, 1915, Wilson MSS, series VI, file 1935, Library of Congress.

40. Hay memoir.

41. For background on the preparedness advocates, see Arthur S. Link, *Woodrow Wilson and the Progressive Era* (New York, 1954), pp. 175–187.

42. Hay memoir.
43. Hay memoir; Memo, Wilson to Burleson, no date, Burleson MSS, vol. 17, Library of Congress; T. W. Gregory to Wilson, February 25, 1916, Wilson MSS, series II, box 94; Johnson Hagood, *The Services of Supply* (Boston, 1927), p. 25; Hagedorn, *Leonard Wood,* II, 174; Hugh L. Scott, *Some Memories of A Soldier* (New York, 1928), p. 469; Memo by Wilson, no date, Burleson MSS, vol. 16.
44. *Congressional Record,* 53:4654, 5348, 5530, 5721, 6202 (March 22, April 3, 5, 8, 15, 1916). "The National Guard under Fire," *Literary Digest,* 52:1132–1133 (April 22, 1916); "Militarism and the Militia," *Scientific American,* new series, 114:396 (April 15, 1916); Wood to E. M. House, April 17, 1916, Wilson MSS, series II, box 96; Scott to Captain F. R. McCoy, April 10, 1916, Scott MSS.
45. General Albert L. Mills to W. F. Sadler, Jr., October 9, 1914, file 011.6, "Revision of the Militia Laws (Pay Bill)," R. G. 168, National Archives.
46. Hay to Albert S. Burleson, July 29, 1915, and Burleson to Wilson, July 31, 1915, Wilson MSS, series VI, file 1935, box 469; Hay to Wilson, November 4, 1915, Wilson MSS, series VI, file 1935, box 469.
47. U.S. Congress, House of Representatives, *Army Reorganization,* Hearings before the Committee on Military Affairs, 66 Cong. (1920), II, 1905.
48. "Bulletin to National Guard Association of the United States, March 18, 1916," (mimeo) and enclosure, file 080, "National Guard Association of the US, Meeting 1916," R. G. 168, National Archives.
49. NGA Convention *Proceedings,* 1917, p. 116.
50. *Congressional Record,* 53:4625 (March 22, 1916).
51. U.S. Congress, House of Representatives, *To Increase the Efficiency of the Military Establishment of the United States,* Hearings before the Committee on Military Affairs, 64 Cong., 1 Sess. (1916), II, 1107.

Chapter III. Years of Stability: 1920–1945

1. *Congressional Record,* 59:5182–5196, 5238–5251, 5275–5291, 5824–5850 (April 5, 6, 7, 19, 1920).
2. NGA Convention *Proceedings,* 1932, p. 13.
3. NGA Convention *Proceedings,* 1939, p. 36; *Congressional Record,* 84:1436, 1439 (February 15, 1939). Information on the strength of the Guard is most conveniently available in the annual *Reports* of the chief of the Militia Bureau (after 1933, the National Guard Bureau).
4. E. Brooke Lee, Jr., *Politics of Our Military National Defense,* S. Doc. 274, 76th Cong., 3 Sess. (1940), p. 130.

5. U.S. Congress, *National Guard Armories*, Joint Hearing before Subcommittees of the Committees on Military Affairs, 74 Cong., 1 Sess. (1935).

6. Richard S. Jones, *A History of the American Legion* (Indianapolis, 1946), p. 248.

7. "Whose National Guard?," *New Republic*, 87:90–91 (June 3, 1936); *Congressional Record*, 83:2381, Appendix (June 6, 1938). Cleveland *Plain Dealer*, October 7, 1937; Cleveland *News*, July 25, 1951.

8. *Creation of the American General Staff, Personal Narrative of the General Staff System of the American Army by Major General William Harding Carter*, S. Doc. 119, 68 Cong., 1 Sess. (1924), p. 58; Elting E. Morison, ed., *The Letters of Theodore Roosevelt*, vol. III: *The Square Deal, 1901–1903* (Cambridge, Mass., 1951), p. 507; *Report of the Secretary of War*, 1908, appendix "g," pp. 145–147.

9. NGA Convention *Proceedings*, 1913, pp. 49–50.

10. U.S. Congress, Senate, *Reorganization of the Army*, Hearings before Subcommittee of the Committee on Military Affairs, 66 Cong., 1 Sess. (1919), pp. 511–541, 1803–1817, 1841–1855, 1887, 1915–1917, 1934; U.S. Congress, House, *Army Reorganization*, Hearings before the Committee on Military Affairs, 66 Cong., 1 and 2 Sess., (1920), II, 1867–1883, 1923; *Congressional Record*, 59:5828–5829 (April 19, 1920).

11. War Department General Orders, No. 6, March 10, 1926; Memo, Lieutenant General W. S. Paul, Director of Personnel and Administration, to Deputy Chief of Staff, "Report of the Committee on Civilian Components, 'Reserve Forces for National Security,'" October 25, 1948, copy at NGA headquarters.

12. Cf. testimony of the chief, Militia Bureau, and NGA president in U.S. Congress, Senate, *War Department Appropriation Bill, 1927*, Hearings before Committee on Appropriations, 69 Cong., 1 Sess. (1926), pp. 189, 203.

13. Interview, General Walsh, April 7, 1960.

14. Milton A. Reckord, Adjutant General of Maryland, to Chief of Staff, April 26, 1929, and Secretary of War to President, April 27, 1929, File AG 321.15 (4–3–29), R. G. 94, National Archives.

15. *U.S. Statutes-at-Large*, 54:885.

16. Adjutants General Association (hereafter, AGA), Mimeographed Transcript of Special Meeting, Washington, D.C., September 1940, pp. 9–11, NGA headquarters.

17. NGA Convention *Proceedings*, 1940, p. 63.

18. File AG 080, "National Guard Assn. of U.S. (1–6–42)," Na-

tional Archives, World War II Records Division, Alexandria, Virginia (hereafter, World War II Archives).

19. The books are John McAuley Palmer, *Statesmanship or War* (Garden City, N.Y., 1927), *Washington, Lincoln, Wilson: Three War Statesmen* (Garden City, N.Y., 1930), and *America in Arms* (New Haven, 1941).

20. Marshall to Palmer, November 13, 1941, Palmer MSS, Library of Congress. On Palmer's contribution to American military policy and the relation between Palmer and Marshall, see Russell F. Weigley, *Towards An American Army* (New York, 1962), ch. 13.

21. Memo by Palmer, "The Place of the National Guard in the Post-War Reserve System," February 22, 1944, Special Planning Division File 325, "National Guard," World War II Archives.

22. Memo, Colonel William E. Carpenter, Legislative & Liaison Branch, General Staff Corps, for Director, Special Planning Division, "Post War Reserve Organization," January 3, 1943 (*sic;* should be 1944), Special Planning Division File 325, "National Guard," World War II Archives.

23. Palmer to Archibald G. Thacher, December 18, 1943, Palmer MSS.

24. U.S. Congress, House, *Proposal to Establish a Single Department of Armed Forces,* Hearings before the Select Committee on Post-War Military Policy, 68 Cong., 2 Sess. (1944), p. 18; *Military Establishment Appropriation Bill for 1944,* Hearings before Subcommittee of Committee on Appropriations, 78 Cong., 1 Sess. (1943), p. 416; *Military Establishment Appropriation Bill for 1946,* Hearings before Subcommittee of Committee on Appropriations, 79 Cong., 1 Sess. (1945), p. 704.

25. "Notes on National Guard Conference," February 28, 1944; Memo for Director, Special Planning Division, from General Palmer, "Conference on Post-War Status of the National Guard, February 28–29, 1944," March 3, 1944; Memo for Chief of Staff from General Tompkins, "Post-War Status of the National Guard," March 8, 1944; all in Special Planning Division File 325, "National Guard," World War II Archives.

26. NGA Convention *Proceedings,* 1943, p. 60; Memo, Tompkins to Chief of Staff, March 8, 1944.

27. Memo for Chief, National Guard Bureau, from Director, Special Planning Division, "The National Guard in the Post-War Period," April 28, 1944, File D-83, O & T, Director of Plans and Operations, ASF, Planning Division, "Organization, Composition and Strength of National Guard—Postwar," World War II Archives; NGA Conference *Proceedings,* 1946, p. 199; Memo, Lieutenant Colonel R. A.

Meredith for Commanding General, AGF, to Chief of Staff, "Post-War Organization of National Guard Ground Forces," July 26, 1944, copy at NGA headquarters; Memo, Tompkins for Chief of Staff, "Post-War National Guard," July 15, 1944, File WDCSA 325, World War II Archives.

28. Palmer, *America in Arms*, pp. 172–173; Memo for the Committee on Civilian Components, January 9, 1948, in vol. 2 of "An Old Soldier's Memories," Palmer MSS.

29. War Department Circular No. 347, August 25, 1944; Memo, Major General Ellard A. Walsh to Adjutants General and Members of the NGA Executive Council, "Post-War Military Policies and Agreements," September 25, 1944, NGA headquarters.

30. Memo for Chief of Staff from General Staff Committee on National Guard Policy, "Post-War National Guard of the United States," September 14, 1944, file WDCSA 325, World War II Archives.

31. Memo for Chief of Staff from Chief, National Guard Bureau, "War Department Policy with Respect to the National Guard," December 27, 1944, file D–83, O & T, Director of Plans and Operations, ASF, Planning Division, "Organization, Composition and Strength of National Guard—Postwar," World War II Archives.

32. Memo for Chief of Staff from General Staff Committee on National Guard Policy, "War Department Policy Concerning Administration of the National Guard," April 17, 1945, same file.

33. The policy statement was never officially published in full. A mimeographed copy is available at NGA headquarters. Portions that applied to the Guard were published in the *Report of the Chief, National Guard Bureau, for the Fiscal Year Ending 30 June 1946*, appendix "O," pp. 309–323.

34. Interview, April 7, 1960.

35. NGA Convention *Proceedings*, 1944, pp. 25–170.

36. NGA Convention *Proceedings*, 1945, pp. 46–47.

37. "Official Proceedings of the Meeting of the Executive Council and Standing Conference, Committees on Policy and Legislation, Camp Ripley-Little Falls, Minnesota, July 27–29, 1944," MS, NGA headquarters. Copies of the agreement with the ROA are at NGA headquarters.

Chapter IV. The Postwar NGA: Portrait of a Successful Lobby

1. U.S. Congress, House, *Special Subcommittee on Reserve Components Hearings on Report on Matters Affecting Civilian Components of the Armed Forces*, Armed Services Committee Serial No. 129, 81 Cong., 1 Sess. (1949), p. 4419.

2. H. N. Willoughby, *Tradition or National Security* (Richmond, Ind., 1947); Major General Harry H. Vaughan, "National Guard and Reserve Must Be United," *The Reserve Officer*, 24:4–5 (October 1947); *New York Times*, September 30, 1947, p. 8; *Reserve Forces for National Security*, Report to the Secretary of Defense by the Committee on Civilian Components, 1948.

3. Interview, April 7, 1960.

4. Memo, Colonel J. W. Cunningham, GSC, for Lieutenant General C. P. Hall, Director of Organization and Training, "Observations Reference the Alleged Feeling Between the Regular Establishment, the National Guard, and the Organized Reserve," April 21, 1947, Organization and Training Division, WDGS, file 325 "(Mar–May 1947)," World War II Archives.

5. Letter, General Walsh to author, November 15, 1960.

6. Forrest C. Pogue, *George C. Marshall: Education of a General, 1880–1939* (New York, 1963), p. 281.

7. All of the differences of opinion over reserve organization, Palmer observed perceptively in 1944, "trace back to differences over the place of the citizen officer." He wrote: "There are, indeed, extreme differences of opinion on this subject. For example, one group with highly organized political support in Congress and the country is contending for the perpetuation of a first reserve component organized in divisions, heretofore commanded, as a rule, by amateur Major Generals. If this extreme view is absurd another equally absurd extreme view is held by some officers in the regular army. Not long ago an experienced army officer told me that, in his opinion, no reserve or 'citizen soldier' should be promoted above the grade of captain in time of peace." Memo for Brigadier General William F. Tompkins, "The 'Citizen Forces' in the Post-War Military Establishment," July 11, 1944, Palmer MSS.

8. NGA Conference *Proceedings*, 1946, p. 199.

9. From a manuscript which, along with other speeches by General Walsh, is at NGA headquarters.

10. As General Martin put it, shortly after he began his second term in the Senate: "Now this matter of the states. We have to get government back toward the courthouses. Now this thing is getting so big here in Washington that I don't believe that there is any man that can master it, unless we start and get a lot of it decentralized, sent back to the state capitals and back to the county courthouses." NGA Executive Council, Meeting, April 25–26, 1953, Transcript, p. 103, NGA headquarters.

11. Official diary of Major General Ellard A. Walsh, entry for June 2, 1947. General Walsh kept this diary for all but the first two of his fourteen years (1944–1957) as NGA president. The diary is

at NGA headquarters, typed and in looseleaf binders. It is a detailed record of Walsh's activities as leader of the NGA.

12. Conference *Proceedings*, p. 156.

13. Paul Memo, 1948.

14. U.S. Congress, Senate, *National Defense Establishment (Unification of the Armed Services)*, Hearings before Committee on Armed Services, 80 Cong., 1 Sess. (1947), p. 706.

15. *Proceedings*, p. 68.

16. H. Rept. 2135, 80 Cong., 2 Sess. (1948), p. 16; on the Guard's objections to armory drill pay for the Reserves, see U.S. Congress, Senate, *Inactive Duty Training Pay*, and *Inactive Duty Training Pay for the Organized Reserve Corps*, Hearings before Subcommittee of the Committee on Armed Services, 80 Cong., 1 Sess. (1947), and U.S. Congress, House, *Military Establishment Appropriations Bill for 1948*, Hearings before Subcommittee of Committee on Appropriations, 80 Cong., 1 Sess. (1947), pp. 1125–1173.

17. *Proceedings*, p. 46.

18. Memo for Director of Personnel and Administration Division, "Report of Visit to the National Guard Association Annual Conference," by Lieutenant Colonel G. E. Baya, GSC, September 24, 1946, Personnel and Administrative Division, WDGS, File 325 "(1 Sep–31 Dec 1944)," World War II Archives.

19. Palmer, *Washington, Lincoln, Wilson*, p. 366.

20. Interview, General Reckord, August 26, 1960. Most of the biographical material about General Reckord is drawn from this interview.

21. AGA Meeting, 1940, Transcript, p. 9.

22. U.S. Congress, House, *Army Organization Bill*, Hearings before Subcommittee, Armed Services Committee Serial No. 187, 81 Cong., 2 Sess. (1950), p. 6158.

23. NGA Conference *Proceedings*, 1946, p. 55.

24. U.S. Congress, House, *Selective Service*, Hearings, Armed Services Committee Serial No. 265, 80 Cong., 2 Sess. (1948), pp. 6526–6550; H. Rept. 1881, 80 Cong., 2 Sess. (1948); S. Rept. 1268, 80 Cong., 2 Sess. (1948); Walsh Diary, March 18–June 19, 1948, esp. May 7.

25. Walsh Diary, January 6, 1949.

26. *Ibid.*, December 18 and 21, 1948.

27. NGA Conference *Proceedings*, 1948, pp. 39–44; *CNGB Report, 1949*, pp. 21–22.

28. Walsh Diary, January 13, 14, 23, and 26, February 12 and 13, 1947; Letter, General Walsh to author, March 19, 1961. On the Bureau's public relations campaign, see *CNGB Report, 1948*, pp.

17–19, and James H. O'Brien, "The Post-War Public Relations Program of the National Guard," unpub. diss. University of Missouri, 1950.

29. Walsh Diary, March 27, 1946, April 8, 1947, February 24 and 27, 1948. General Walsh commented, upon reading this in manuscript: "Your conclusions in re UMT and the Guard are completely logical. Between the American Legion, War Department, Senators Taft, Wilson, Thye, and the Minnesota congressional delegation, the going was often times rugged and decidedly unpleasant."

30. Walsh Diary, March 31, 1948.

31. Ibid., October 28, 1948.

32. Ibid., October 1, 1946.

33. Ibid., October 18, November 1, November 15, 1949; see also New York Times, December 3, 1949, p. 3.

34. Walsh Diary, June 20 and 26, 1946.

35. Ibid., December 18, 1948; U.S. Congress, House, Hearings before the Full Committee on the Bill to Authorize the Composition of the Army of the United States and the Air Force of the United States and for Other Purposes, Armed Services Committee Serial No. 12, 81 Cong., 1 Sess. (1949), p. 275.

36. NGA Conference Proceedings, 1949, p. 75.

37. Walsh Diary, August 26, 1948.

38. U.S. Congress, House, Military Establishment Appropriations Bill for 1947, Hearings before Subcommittee of Committee on Appropriations, 70 Cong., 2 Sess. (1946), p. 1150.

39. Proceedings, p. 34.

Chapter V. Years of Defense: The Cold War

1. According to the NGA, the states furnish about $50 million a year to the Guard. New York Times, May 20, 1962. That would be about 6 percent of government expenditures for the Guard. According to Secretary of Defense Robert S. McNamara, the states contribute about 3 percent. New York Times, July 4, 1962.

2. See the excellent analysis in Samuel P. Huntington, The Common Defense (New York, 1961), chs. 1, 2.

3. For a criticism of the trend, see Maxwell D. Taylor, The Uncertain Trumpet (New York, 1959).

4. Semiannual Report of the Secretary of Defense, January 1 to June 30, 1953, pp. 67–68; U.S. Congress, House of Representatives, Review of the Reserve Program, Hearings, Armed Services Committee Serial No. 22, 85 Cong., 1 Sess. (1957), p. 706.

5. U.S. Congress, House, Full Committee Hearing on H. R. 5426, Armed Services Committee Serial No. 49, 82 Cong., 1 Sess. (1951), p. 1968.

6. Army Regulation 11–1, December 31, 1956.

7. Timothy W. Stanley, *American Defense and National Security* (Washington, 1956), p. 124n.; U.S. Congress, House, *National Reserve Plan*, Hearings, Armed Services Committee Serial No. 11, 84 Cong., 1 Sess. (1955), *passim;* National Security Training Commission, *20th Century Minutemen, A Report to the President on A Reserve Forces Training Program,* December 1, 1953; Office of Defense Mobilization, *Manpower Resources for National Security,* A Report to the President, January 6, 1954; U.S. Congress, House, *Review of the Reserve Program,* Hearings, Armed Services Committee Serial No. 22, 85 Cong., 1 Sess. (1957), pp. 665–666, 686, 692, 713, 772–773, 825.

8. *Congressional Record,* 108:10352 (June 13, 1962).

9. Cf. Louis Smith, *American Democracy and Military Power* (Chicago, 1951), pp. 305–315.

10. U.S. Congress, House, *Review of the Reserve Program,* Hearings, Armed Services Committee Serial No. 72, 86 Cong., 2 Sess. (1960), p. 6526.

11. Interview, September 11, 1959.

12. AGA, 1952 Annual Meeting, Transcript, part II, p. 284, NGA headquarters. Payments to the NGA are undoubtedly subsidized by some state governments. For example, the state code of Arizona provides that the adjutant general "may belong to the national association and other organizations for the betterment of the national guard, and may subscribe for and obtain periodicals, literature and magazines of such other organizations, and pay dues and charges therefor from funds of the state appropriated for that purpose." *Arizona Revised Statutes* (1956), Title 26, Sec. 103.

13. Indications of patronage were evident in a dispute in 1961 between the governor and the adjutant general of Mississippi. The governor was trying to force the adjutant general to restore a Guard major to a full-time job as maintenance supervisor of an Air National Guard unit. The adjutant general was resisting. New Orleans *Times-Picayune,* May 9, 1961.

14. *New York Times,* July 6, 1962.

15. U.S. Congress, House, *Department of the Army Appropriations for 1957,* Hearings before Subcommittee of Committee on Appropriations, 84 Cong., 2 Sess. (1956), p. 1572. General Walsh replied, "Well, Tony was unable to be here." The answer may have been disingenuous. General Anthony J. Drexel Biddle, member of a socially prominent Philadelphia family, athlete, diplomat, former Reserve officer of the Army and, at the time of his death, Kennedy's ambassador to Spain, was appointed adjutant general of Pennsylvania in 1955 without having served in the Guard, and he was not

an enthusiastic participant in NGA affairs. The NGA may not have invited him to be there.

16. Interview with Paul J. Kilday, judge of the United States Court of Military Appeals and formerly a member of the House Armed Services Committee, October 11, 1962.

17. On the governors' activity, see, for example: *State Government*, 31:158–162 (Summer 1958); U.S. Congress, House, *Proposed Reduction in the Strength of the National Guard*, Hearings, Armed Services Committee Serial No. 77, 85 Cong., 2 Sess. (1958), pp. 5816–5857; U.S. Congress, Senate, *Department of Defense Appropriations for 1959*, Hearings before Subcommittee of Committee on Appropriations, 85 Cong., 2 Sess. (1958), pp. 1354–1359, 1364–1365.

18. *Proceedings*, p. 209.

19. *Congressional Record*, 108:7540–7541 (May 2, 1962).

20. Interview, November 30, 1960.

21. *Congressional Record*, 104:14489 (July 21, 1958).

22. *Congressional Record*, 108:10357 (June 13, 1962).

23. U.S. Congress, House, *Military Reserve Posture Hearings*, Armed Services Committee Serial No. 66, 87 Cong., 2 Sess. (1962), p. 6173.

24. Interview, March 25, 1960. Comparison with the ROA illustrates the superiority of the Guard's internal communications. In 1958 a member of the House Defense Appropriations Subcommittee, attempting to elicit from the chief, Army Reserve and ROTC Affairs (Reserve counterpart of the National Guard Bureau chief) a statement in support of higher Reserve strength, referred to an earlier statement before the subcommittee by ROA President deLesseps S. Morrison. The chief replied that he was "not aquainted with the testimony. I do not know just what General Morrison's testimony was," he added. Such things simply do not happen to the National Guard. House, *Department of Defense Appropriations for 1959* (Department of the Army), Hearings (1958), p. 164.

25. U.S. Congress, House, *Military Posture Briefing*, Armed Services Committee Serial No. 16, 86 Cong., 1 Sess. (1959), p. 865.

26. Interview with Robert B. Smart, October 11, 1962.

27. Cf. Morris Janowitz, *The Professional Soldier* (Glencoe, Ill., 1960), p. 356. Janowitz asserts that Congress has opposed unification of the armed services for fear that unification would weaken the balance between the executive and legislative branches of government. "It has feared overconcentration of military power, and has looked to interservice rivalry as a source of information and as a basis for civilian intervention in military affairs." Congress likes to preserve the autonomy of the Guard for similar reasons. See also

Huntington's analysis of Congress' role in military affairs, *The Soldier and the State*, pp. 400–427.

28. *Time*, 63:18 (March 1, 1954).

29. Interview with Bryce N. Harlow, April 13, 1960.

30. "Presentation of Major General Ellard A. Walsh . . . at a Special Closed Meeting of the Adjutants General . . . and General Officers of the Line of the Army National Guard, Washington, D.C., 23 Jan. 1957," MS at NGA headquarters (hereafter, "Presentation . . . 23 Jan. 1957").

31. Washington *Post and Times-Herald*, January 16, 1957.

32. "Presentation . . . 23 Jan. 1957."

33. U.S. Congress, House, *Proposed Reduction in the Strength of the National Guard*, pp. 5648, 5866ff.

34. Walsh Diary, February 26, 1957.

35. *New York Times*, January 15, 1957.

36. Walsh Diary, February 5, 1957; U.S. Congress, House, *Memorandum of Agreement by Subcommittee No. 1 on Requirement for 6 Months' Training for National Guard Enlistees . . .*, Armed Services Committee Serial No. 15, 85 Cong., 1 Sess. (1957).

37. Interview with Robert B. Smart, April 14, 1960. For a discussion of the constitutional issue, see Huntington, *The Soldier and the State*, pp. 426–427.

38. Huntington, *The Common Defense*, pp. 139–143.

39. House, *Military Posture Briefing* (1959), p. 847; see also Vinson's statement in U.S. Congress, House, *Department of Defense Appropriations for 1959* (Advanced Research Projects Agency et al.), Hearings before Subcommittee of Committee on Appropriations, 85 Cong., 2 Sess. (1958), pp. 1042 ff.

40. *Congressional Record*, 105:15109 (August 4, 1959).

41. *Congressional Record*, 108:20517 (September 24, 1962).

42. U.S. Congress, House, *Full Committee Consideration of House Joint Resolution 876, To Authorize the President to Order Units and Members in the Ready Reserve to Active Duty for Not More than 12 Months, and For Other Purposes*, Hearings, Armed Services Committee Serial No. 74, 87 Cong., 2 Sess. (1962), p. 7143.

43. John F. Stennis of Mississippi in *Congressional Record*, 108:10358 (June 13, 1962).

44. U.S. Congress, House, *Military Reserve Posture*, Report of Subcommittee No. 3, Armed Services Committee Serial No. 70, 87 Cong., 2 Sess. (1962), p. 6671.

45. The anguish that the issue caused the NGA is illustrated by an entry in General Walsh's diary (February 22, 1953): "It is apparent that an impasse has been reached involving two irrecon-

cilable points of view, and both of which, conceivably, are right. On one hand there is the point of view expressed by New York and others that if the Guard is to be ready on 'M-day' and accomplish its Federal missions, it must have trained men. This is axiomatic and there can be no quarrel on that score. On the other hand there is the point of view expressed by Maryland, Mississippi, Georgia, and the solid South that the Guard should adhere to the traditional volunteer system, and who is there to say this is not right for it is the system which has made the Guard what it is . . . The Association is further handicapped in that it has no knowledge as to whether the Governors . . . desire the authority to requisition on the President for trained men or what will be the attitude of the Pentagon and Congress. All in all it is a very troublesome situation and it would be well for all concerned to proceed cautiously."

46. *Congressional Record,* daily ed., July 2, 1963, pp. 11428–11429.

47. National Guard Association, Meeting of the Executive Council, April 25–26, 1953, transcript, p. 312, NGA headquarters.

48. U.S. Congress, Senate, *Armed Forces Reserve Act,* Hearings before Subcommittee of the Committee on Armed Services, 82 Cong., 2 Sess. (1952), pp. 104–130.

49. Walsh Diary, May 22, 1952, and NGA Conference *Proceedings,* 1952, pp. 266 ff.

50. Walsh Diary, March 21, 1955.

51. *Ibid.,* May 27, 1955.

52. *Ibid.,* July 13, 1955.

53. NGA, Executive Council Meeting, 1953, Transcript, p. 295. The only published background of the schism is in the NGA Conference *Proceedings,* 1952, pp. 163–175.

54. Adjutants General Association, 1957 Annual Meeting, stenographic transcript, NGA Headquarters.

55. Walsh Diary, February 18, 1957.

INDEX

Achievements, definition of, 13–14
Adjutants general: functions, 2, 99, 155n.; domination of NGA, 4, 30; as lobbyists for NGA, 100–101; appointments of as patronage, 125
Adjutants General Association, 70, 71, 137
Aiken, George, 117
Ainsworth, Fred C., 34, 35, 53, 94
Air Force, Department of: conflicts with Guard, 73–74, 90, 98–99, 104–105; assistant chief of staff for reserve components, 115
American Legion, 81, 95; as ally of Guard, 51; as sponsor of universal military training, 64, 71, 101, 103
Antimilitarism, in Congress, 21, 31, 35, 37, 42, 45, 120, 165
Appropriations Committee(s), 129–130, 153; subcommittees of, 63, 83–84, 127–130, 146–147; in House, 100, 146, 150, 156
Armed Forces Reserve Act of 1952, 112–113, 124; preparation of, 118; NGA opposition to, 155–157
Armed Services Committee(s), 83, 127, 129, 147, 151, 153; in House, 97, 128, 146, 154; in Senate, 86, 125, 128, 155–156; subcommittees of, 151
Army, United States. *See* Army, Department of; Regular Army; War Department
Army, Department of: action on Gray Board report, 105; issues six-months' training directive, 113, 118–119, 138–139; assistant chief of staff for reserve components, 115–116; as political ally of Guard, 139, 144–145, 151–152; appeals to NGA for help, 158

Army and Air Force Authorization Act of 1949, 74
Army and Air Force Vitalization and Equalization Retirement Act of 1948, 73
Army and Navy Journal, 17, 22
Assistant Secretary of Defense (Manpower, Personnel, and Reserves), Office of, 115

Baker-March bill, 45
Baker, Newton D., 38
Baldwin, Hanson, 125
Baldwin, Raymond E., 86
Biddle, Anthony J. Drexel, 127
Boyle, Leo M., 123
Bricker, John W., 117
Bridges, Styles, 86
Brooks, Overton, 132
Brucker, Wilber M., 139
Budget Bureau, United States, 102, 134
Burleson, Albert S., 37
Byrd, Harry F., 86

Cantwell, James F., 128n.
Chamberlain, George, 38–39
Chicago Tribune, 81
Chief of Staff, Office of (Army), 88–89
Chiperfield, Burnett M., 41
CIO (Congress of Industrial Organizations), 52
Civil War, 15; veterans of in Guard, 17
Clark, Bennett Champ, 63
Clark, Grenville, 58, 96
Cleveland Chamber of Commerce, 52
Cleveland, Grover, 21
Collins, J. Lawton, 97, 150
Collins, Ross, 150
Congress, United States: indifference to military affairs, 20, 48;

HARVARD POLITICAL STUDIES